*Past and Pending*

"To tell a life's story in poetry requires a deft touch, emotional range, and endless human bravery. Sasha Chinnaya's poems range from 'A Symphony of Curry,' which beats on the page like a 'tireless heart,' to portraits of New York's pandemic year, in which 'parting is all we know' and 'uncertainty blooms like a new love.' Her poems show a poet's sensitivity to changing places, people, and the impersonal forces that shape and structure our lives."

—STEVE MENTZ
*Professor of English, St. John's University*

"In this highly insightful work of art, Chinnaya reveals her story by bringing us on a journey by first treasuring the beauty within our childhood, then acknowledging the complexities of adulthood—and that together they ultimately help us to understand ourselves and make us who we are."

—DANIELLE N. ROMAIN
*Book lover*

"Sasha Chinnaya's writing is moving as she recounts the stages of her life, from childhood through adulthood, with vivid poems. Her work is deeply introspective and raw as she chronicles the joys of making cultural dishes with loved ones, the sorrow of feeling like an outsider, the uncertainty that young people face when their futures are not clearly carved out, and more."

—OLIVIA SINGH
*Senior entertainment reporter*

"Each of the poems within this collection is so beautiful, exciting, memorable, and enjoyable to read. I just couldn't stop reading. I loved the way Chinnaya described her childhood, and the different cultural foods made me very hungry. It was adorable and engaging to read about her husky pet and all of his mischief and things he liked to do. Some of my favorite poems include 'Capitalism Never Sleeps,' 'Home,' 'Fall,' 'Husky,' and 'Pastries at Martha's.'"

—ENA CHINNAYA
*Book lover*

# *Past and Pending*

Poems of Nostalgia and Endurance

## Sasha Chinnaya

RESOURCE *Publications* • Eugene, Oregon

PAST AND PENDING
Poems of Nostalgia and Endurance

Copyright © 2021 Sasha Chinnaya. All rights reserved. Except for brief quotations in critical publications or reviews, no part of this book may be reproduced in any manner without prior written permission from the publisher. Write: Permissions, Wipf and Stock Publishers, 199 W. 8th Ave., Suite 3, Eugene, OR 97401.

Resource Publications
An Imprint of Wipf and Stock Publishers
199 W. 8th Ave., Suite 3
Eugene, OR 97401

www.wipfandstock.com

PAPERBACK ISBN: 978-1-6667-1086-1
HARDCOVER ISBN: 978-1-6667-1087-8
EBOOK ISBN: 978-1-6667-1088-5

AUGUST 16, 2021

For my parents, my brother Luke and our dearly beloved dog Damin. In the most trying times, there is always hope when you're surrounded by the warmth that comes from loved ones.

# Contents

*List of Illustrations/Photos:* | x

*Chapter 1*
THE VIVID NOSTALGIA OF CHILDHOOD YEARS | 1

What Happened To Her? | 2
Star Gal | 4
That Nineties Child | 5
Mithai | 7
A Symphony of Curry | 9
Dhal | 11
Liberty Ave. | 13
Life In The City | 14
Sabrina | 16
Summer Road Trip | 18
Immigrant Identity | 20
Grandma | 23
Ice Block | 25
Fishing | 26
Swing | 27
Spinning Chair | 28
The Hospital | 29
Closer Than A Role
Model | 32
Mama | 33
The Lost Garden | 34
Life Before Kindergarten | 36

*Chapter 2*
SCHOOL DAYS IN PASSING | 37

Kindergarten | 40
Kindergarten Graduation | 41
Assumption | 43
Schoolyard Games | 44
Halloween At School | 45
Book Fair | 47
What I Miss About Elementary
School | 48
Frizzy Hairs | 49
Wish I Knew | 51
Music Recital | 52
Too Quiet? | 54

The Year 2008 | 55
Announcement | 56
Funeral In Canada | 57
Recess | 59
Eighth Grade | 60
Two Worlds | 61
High School Freshman | 63
Fire In The Attic | 64
Subway Rides | 66
Yearbook Of Memories | 68

Gratitude For Parents | 70
High School Years | 73
Purchase Road | 75
Library Cages | 77
The Stood | 78
What Do I Say? | 80
Changes In College | 82
What Comes Next | 83
Writing With I | 84
English As A Major | 86

*Chapter 3*
ARTIST IN PROGRESS | 90

Wanderer | 93
Never Enough | 95
Saturday Stress | 97
Let It Go | 99
Sad | 100
Words and Power | 101
Tough Skin | 102
For Women Of Color | 103

Art Takes Time | 106
Is That A Valid Career? | 107
Golden Times | 108
Untouchable | 110
Lasting Relics | 111
Work It Out | 112
Balance | 113

*Chapter 4*
PARTING IS ALL WE KNOW | 114

Upon A Dream, Once | 117
Ghost | 119
Raw | 120
Pages Torn Between Us | 121
Excuses | 122
Denial | 123

If People Care | 125
Parting Is All We Know | 126
Just Say It's Over | 127
Re-defining | 128
Nonchalant | 129
Relationship Like Clay | 130

*Chapter 5*
REFLECTIONS THROUGH A PANDEMIC | 131

Conveniences | 132
Career Crisis | 133

Love Is On My Mind | 134
Green To The Bone | 136

Capitalism Never Sleeps | 139
Toxic Office | 141
Millennial | 142
Social Activism, Social Media | 144
Uncertainty Blooms | 146
Too Much Thinking | 149
Anytime I Get Sad | 150
Shoes Not Used | 152
Spring Birthday | 154
Anxiety, An Old Friend | 156
Another Day | 158
Earth Day | 160
Reading Through A Crisis | 161
Pastries At Martha's | 163
Home | 164
Halloween | 167
Fall | 168
Husky | 171
Instagram Eye View | 174
Open Road | 175
Endurance | 176

## List of Illustrations/Photos:

That Nineties Child | 5
Mithai | 7
Dhal | 11
The Lost Garden | 34
Halloween At School | 45
Subway Rides | 66
Yearbook Of Memories | 68
Purchase Road | 75
Wanderer | 93
Never Enough | 95
Is That A Valid Career? | 107
Upon A Dream, Once | 117
Spring Birthday | 154
Husky | 171

*Chapter 1*

# The Vivid Nostalgia of Childhood Years

CHILDHOOD IS AN UNCOMFORTABLE time, but it's also special. We don't realize how fleeting it is until we become adults. Imagination, fantasy, and naïve thinking intermingles with real experiences and people we encounter. Family, places, trends, friends, and the events that take place stay with us throughout our lives. It's the foundation from which we build our lives and not all of it is easy. Even in childhood, there are weights of emotion, struggles, partings, betrayals, confusion and a feeling that no matter what we do, we don't belong. There are places from childhood that feel familiar and safe even if they no longer exist because they still linger in our memories. These places can be a vacation spot with loved ones or a garden that has since been demolished. Home is not always just the house that we live in, but the people we are surrounded by, the spicy scents in the kitchen, and the music we listen to on long drives.

    I look back at my childhood fondly because I felt protected and loved. I'm thankful for the memories, but I know that everyone's childhood is different and some people have that safety ripped away at too young an age. Traumas happen everyday at large and small scales and we can never anticipate when our life is about to change forever. All we can do is keep moving forward, find new dreams to aspire to, create new homes, make new relationships, and swing higher even if we're afraid of falling. The vivid nostalgia of the past is always there to turn back to when we need it.

## What Happened To Her?

There was this little girl.
She was so proud of her curls,
Her hips, and her brown skin.
She never felt pressure to be thin.

She loved her home
And her body
The way it was.
She didn't know how much her life
Would change every year
Or how she'd learn more about herself
And still always be discovering greater truths.
What happened to Her?

She had so many dreams,
She thought she would conquer the world
Through any of the many
Different career paths she envisioned:
Hairstylist, psychologist, fashion designer,
Film director, chef, or fiction writer.

She knew all these opportunities she had.
She never settled on one direct path,
But followed a long and winding road
Of twists, turns and adventure,
And this little girl,
Oh how she loved to twirl
And mimic intricate dances
From her favorite Indian movies.
What happened to her?

What happened to the dancing,
The physical connection to the music,

Without care of who was watching?
All that spinning and whining,
It was her means of expression,
Her own special way of finding
Her identity,
Despite any narrow-minded mentalities.
The bangles would clash
As she shook her hands.
Her arms would move with the rhythm.
What happened to Her?

Her odd way of thinking
Became too in depth
For most people her age
And they all thought her rather strange.
The world mistook
Her quiet ways
For a lack of effort.
The way she shook
Her hips became a good laugh
As people deduced her beauty,
Talked about her weight
And picked apart her body.
It's as if she wasn't a little girl at all,
But just a doll.
An object for people to throw opinions at.
What happened to Her?

She used to be the light of the party,
A force of nature who never tired
Or grew sad and bitter.
When she danced, she felt everything.
She understood much more
Than the world gave her credit for.

## Star Gal

She's a star gal.
Her life is better than a movie,
Because she writes her own story
And speaks her mind
Without fear of being disliked.
Her face lights up like the moon.
Not the sun?
No, not as obvious
Or fiery yet.

First, she's calm,
Observant and wisely thinking
About her life and the world around her,
But there's beauty
And power in her dance.
It was her first form of expression,
Of art and creativity,
But certainly not her last
Because she keeps growing in knowledge.
When she moves and twirls,
Shakes her wrists
And smiles wide
With light in her eyes,
She captures the world's attention.

# That Nineties Child

Colorful patterns,
Geometric shapes,
Black clothing and lipstick,
Stacks of VHS tapes.

Indian movies with subtitles;
I knew the songs by heart.
Same movies I recycle,
Rewinding the tapes to the start.

I used to mimic the dances.
I used to picture
I was the star gal.
Emotion in every glance.
I used to wear this deep green shawl,
And spin and feel
The beat of the songs.

Ring pops and fruit rollups,
*Rugrats, Looney Toones,*

Cartoon Network and *Scooby-Doo*.
Boybands, pop music,
And watching TV at its peak,
Way before it was on a phone screen.

My best friend had braces.
Lipliner and grunge weren't weak.
Coffee shops were bustling.
Coney Island was the special place to be,
Where I'd walk on the beach
With my parents always protecting me.
A nineties child remembers it all.
Old memories keep on rustling
Like a colorful, rotating disco ball.

# Mithai

Mithai always makes me smile.
Those triangular shaped pastries
Bring on so many fond memories
Of birthday parties, services, weddings,
And other celebrations.
Mithai is one of those sweets
That I'd probably never buy in a bakery
Because I'm so used to loved ones making it
For me.
I'm used to watching the process
With excitement and glee
As the rich scents
Of coconut, nutmeg and almond essence
Fill the kitchen.

My aunt makes some
Of the best mithai.
It's never too sweet though.
She cuts the dough,
After rolling it in all those fragrant spices.
She heats the pot with oil
And she fries it on the stove.
Bubbles form around it
And my mouth waters for a taste.
The mithai browns and swells
And my aunt turns off that simmering heat.
She creates another mixture in a smaller bowl
With food coloring and powdered sugar.
She separates that glazing sugar
Into bowls of blue, pink and red,
And any other colors to spread over the fried dough.
It dries and hardens
And then we eat it together.

## A Symphony of Curry

A big pot would be on the stove.
My mom, my aunt or my grandma
Would be hovering over it,
Stirring with a steel spoon.
It's not that the men don't cook.
They know spices too.
They can curate a delicious meal
Just as good.
They just don't.
Don't ask me *why not?*
Ask them.

I don't know a recipe for curry.
I don't know measurements for curry.
I know the scent, the ingredients,
The flavor, the childhood nostalgia,
The art of creating it;
Of eating fish curry with mangoes,
Chicken curry with potatoes,
Crab curry with coconut milk,
And white rice always on the side;
The curry gravy spreading on the rice,
Mixing into it, absorbing,
Flowing together in harmony.

These spices blend in a perfect balance,
An aromatic symphony of garlic,
And curry powder.
Our kitchen always felt warm this way.
It was alive and complete
Like a tireless heart,
Meticulously beating away.

# Dhal

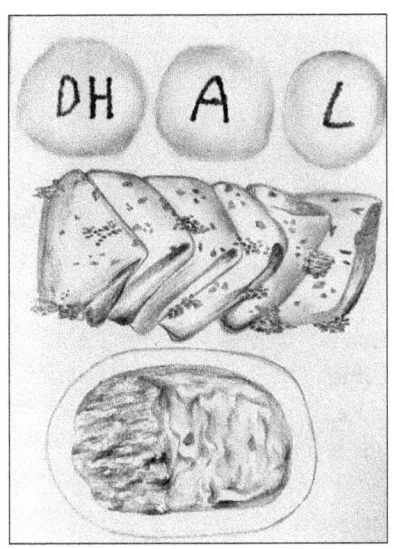

It's a warm, soothing pool
On a bed of white rice.
Sometimes, it fills a vast desert of crisp, rich roti
That is flaky, tasty, and made from scratch.
We almost never buy plain roti.
We only buy dhal puri
When my grandmother isn't making it.

Grinding dhal peas was always fun.
I used to play outside and watch my grandma
Grind those dhal peas in the sun,
With tables set up and fresh breeze around us.
I remember churning the peas
Inside that silver machine
Until they were refined as powder.

When it isn't being grinded

And stuffed into balls of dough,
The dhal peas are heated on the stove.
Some people like it thin,
Others like it thick
So it absorbs into the rice well.
When you eat it,
You inhale that wonderful smell.

My parents used to eat dhal
With pumpkin on the side.
Dhal and rice was also
One of the few things
My little brother ate.
So, my mom made it for him
Most of the time
Because he was so picky with every type of food.

There's this old Guyanese saying:
"Dhal and rice make coolie bai nice."
We used to sing that to my brother
Whenever he was eating it.
Those memories make me laugh
And shake my head to this day.

## Liberty Ave.

Train tracks above,
Drilling away as we stroll.
Between that gritty sound, the crowded streets,
And good prices on greens you can't beat,
There is so much excitement that awaits.
I'll always know exactly where I am
On Liberty Avenue with cars passing by,
Blasting Indian music,
And honking endlessly
Through the traffic.
I'm waiting for my mom
Outside the fish market.
The scent of fish was too strong inside.
The McDonald's that my dad
Used to take my brother and I to
For breakfast before school some mornings;
The library where my mom brought us
To get summer reading books.
The street where my cousins lived,
The sweet smelling flower shop,
The Little Guyana Bakery.
These places still exist.
We'd always go to the Indian movie store,
Which is what I would call this store
That sold electronics and Indian movies.
I never looked at the sign above
Because I always knew where to find it.
It was a place of endless possibilities;
New VHS tapes and DVDs to add
To my growing collection.

## Life In The City

Taking the train with my mom,
In the mornings,
At the crack of dawn,
As she went to work.
Sometimes, my little brother
Would come with us
And we'd all travel to the city.
An adventure, a routine;
Unforgettable sites to be seen.
Walking under the turnstile,
When I was still small enough
To sneak through.
The adults used to use token coins
Instead of metro cards.
I loved hearing the sound of the coins
Hitting the slots,
Like some kind of machine game
Or a toy I wanted to understand.
No time to stop and stare!
People were walking fast
And mom always kept us close
And told us to be alert
For any dangers that might pass.

My favorite part of being on the J train
Was looking out the window
And seeing sunlight hit water
With the city buildings in the backdrop,
As we crossed the Williamsburg Bridge.
Mom always knew the best spots
For breakfast and snacks.
Once we loaded up,
We went to her office.

As she worked,
My brother and I would play.
He had his toy cars
And I had coloring books.
There were rules about where
We could stay
And how far we could wander.
The office space seemed much larger
When I was a kid.
After work, the real fun would start.
Mom took us to Kmart
Where the best toys awaited
And there was a store next to it
That sold delicious popcorn in tins.
Sometimes, we'd go see a movie too
Or go to the circus if it was around.
The chaos of Times Square never phased us.
To city kids, the glare of lights
Was enchanting and exciting.
The crowds of people meant
Something important was happening.
The salty, greasy foods of New York City
Were comforting treats only to be had once in a while.
The tall, towering buildings
Made us feel like we had entered
A magical land or amusement park.
By the end of the day,
We'd be exhausted
Coming home on multiple trains.
Yet, we had the best day,
Spending time in our city
And these are memories
I'll always be grateful for.

## Sabrina

I don't remember when
We became good friends.

You had a bright smile.
You liked red starbursts,
Ate very little food,
And you knew how to prevent things
From getting worse
With your supportive words.
You liked to watch movies
And get into trouble.
Life was never boring
With you around.

You were always friendly
And kind to me.
Even before I started kindergarten,
I had a friend in you.
We used to study the dances
From Indian movies
And then dance as closely
As we could to the real thing.

We used to watch *Sabrina The Teenage Witch*.
We joked that you were named after her.
We watched the animated version
And the one with Melissa Joan Hart.
I always think I was so alone,
So in my own world and zone.
I was always a quiet kid.
You were popular and friendly.
We were opposite ends of a spectrum,
Held together by common family members,

And separated by small changes throughout time.
I never said goodbye
Because we never decided to part.
We just went in different directions
And drifted apart slowly.
I don't know when it all ended.
Maybe we never said goodbye?
How was it that someone who was there
So early on in my life
Is no longer here like so many people
Who passed through my life?

I met you again at a funeral.
Your face was the same.
We shook hands and smiled.
I hadn't genuinely smiled that wide
In a very long time.
It was like time hadn't changed.
We both still remembered everything.

## Summer Road Trip

Summer heat, frizzy hair,
Long, noisy road trips
Back and forth
Between Canada and New York
Over the years.

Madonna's "La Isla Bonita" playing in the van
On a strange mixed CD,
Which also included reggae,
Hip-hop, and Caribbean music.
I remember many details
And still forget the words we said.
I remember driving
Till we reached my uncle's house.
It was always the place we'd stay.
I remember dancing at a family party,
The reggae music blasting,
But I didn't notice the humor.
Their laughter was rising like flames
Targeted at me.

Yellow shirt and pants skirt;
Bad combination;
Noticed a little too late.
Nothing could save me
From the humiliation game.
I was known for dancing in those days.
Except, my body was never thin.
I had a belly
And that night it showed.

Someone told me to wear that outfit.
I don't remember who.

I wish there were some things
I never knew,
Like that people don't care
If you're a naïve child.
They'll treat you like an adult,
Gossiping about your body and style,
Anything for a good laugh;
Never mind how old.

## Immigrant Identity

I remember my family
Throwing parties in the yard.
So many people were there.
Yet, still I felt apart
From everything and everyone.
My cousins were older.
Their lives always appeared
Interesting and full of movement.
Except, their lives were also colder,
Plagued with great misfortunes;
Things I couldn't see clearly
When I was younger.

Their houses were smaller.
Where they lived
Was always changing.
They were born in Guyana.
That shouldn't have made a difference.
Yet, it did.

How strange that I've never
Been to the country
That my family came from.
All I have are the stories:
Some good, some bad,
Some funny, and some sad.
It must've been tough
For my cousins to come
Into this country and fit in
When they lived a good portion
Of younger years in Guyana.
Schools must've been different
As well as the environment, the transportation,

The foods and the interactions.
They'd never say it,
But there must've been
Many cultural clashes
And few places to vent.

All I know is I used to wish
I was more like them.
Their lives were glistening
With excitement and adventure.
They were popular,
Attracting people like magnets.
Their friends would come over to our house
When we threw birthday parties.
I always felt too shy
To hang out with the older kids.
They were too cool.
There were always games
With basketballs and frisbees.
We played freeze tag and card games;
Anything to pass the time.

I thought that my cousins' lives were golden.
I didn't see how much more
My brother and I had.
We had a safe home
That wasn't always changing.
Both our parents were working,
But we always had someone
To pick us up from school.
We had a whole backyard to play in.
I always felt safe.
We were both born in the U.S.A.
I've always been told

That it's a privilege to be born here.
Not better or worse,
Just a privilege
I've taken for granted.
To not have to go through a terrifying process,
To not have to wait with fear of being caught,
To not have to marry
To make it to "the land of opportunity."

## Grandma

I always think of grandma
When I smell
Bengay and vicks,
Plantain soup boiling on the stove,
Hot tea brewing
With a side of saltine crackers,
Pine tarts and cross buns
Cooking in the oven,
And moth balls in her closet.
Those scents are the best kind
Of nostalgia.

My grandma is unique,
Unlike any other grandma
I've ever seen.
She had a chicken farm in Guyana
Where she raised five children
And earned the daily bread for her household.
She is a Christian not just in title,
But in heart and soul;
Through words and deeds.
She used to welcome beggars
Into her house in Guyana
And gave them food to eat.
She makes the best dhal purri.
She lost her mom very young
And was forced to marry at the age of sixteen.
She had to grow up too fast,
But she made the most
Out of what she had.

I remember grandma
Traveling to and from New Jersey

At late hours for her job.
There, she used to babysit
These white kids.
Sometimes, I felt jealous
Because my grandma was
With these kids so often.
It felt like she was their grandma too
And I wasn't excited to share her.
Yet, grandma has always embodied generosity.
A few of the many things
I've learned from her
Are humility and kindness.

To this day,
Grandma loves watching wrestling each week.
She is one of the most hardworking
People I know;
Always waking up early to
Do more work.
She loves wearing pearls
And is picky with most things,
But her love knows no bounds.
Everything good inside her
Is what she also passed down
To my mom.
I hope I can be more
Like her and my mom
As I get older
Because they've both set the bar quite high.

## Ice Block

It's also known as custard block;
Light golden yellow
With an orange hue.
It's like ice cream
Or some popsicle of rich flavor
In the form of ice cubes.
My grandma used to make it.
She made some pans of the custard
And put it in the oven to bake.
She poured the other half
Into ice trays and
Any containers we could spare.
I ate it mostly during summer.
It was always a delicacy,
But eating it with my family
Made it all the more rich.

# Fishing

We are fishing at a lake,
Waiting to go home.
Fishing is not the break
I had planned for a summer vacation.

Water is still and sunlight gleams.
Everything is not as it seems.
My family smiles
When they catch a big fish.
I start screaming and can't wait to ditch.
The fish falls on the wood,
A few inches from my feet.
It's wobbling, shaking, struggling for its life.
I never thought I'd understand that feeling
Until I reached age twenty-five.

My aunt showed me there was nothing
To be afraid of.
She cleaned the fish right in front of me
And then fried it with seasoning.
We ate delicious fish sandwiches that night.

Back then, I was still so full of fright
Of this big fish out of water!
Now, I feel sorry for the fish.
I can relate to all the drama
Of entering a place you don't belong.

## Swing

I thought I could do anything
When I was a kid,
Smiling and soaring on a swing.
Swinging high up
Made me feel like I could fly
Like the birds gliding in the sky.
That yellow house
And the faces around me
Evaporated as I played on the swing.
At a certain point in life,
People stop swinging high.
It starts to feel too silly
To dream that big
Or to take a risk and try.
Failure looms like rain clouds,
Forcing you to flee inside.
You say goodbye to the swing
And start to stress over every little thing.
What you love starts to feel
Like a waste of time.

## Spinning Chair

When I was a kid,
I fell off a spinning chair;
One of the clumsiest things I ever did.
My head had a tear
Because I hit it real bad
On the edge of a counter.
I made it to the doctor in time,
Thanks to my dad.
Otherwise, the damage
Might have been too severe.

I had to get stitches;
I'm sure it hurt,
But I don't remember the pain.
I was spinning so fast
It felt like wind in my hair;
My own Coney Island ride.

When you're spinning that fast
It almost feels like a swing
Where you can't feel
Your feet touch the ground.
So, you're basically flying.

I remember a scar on my forehead
For years after.
When light hit the scar,
Then I could see it.
Otherwise, I only remembered
The moment from what others
Told me about it.
Funny how even memories
Can change over time.

## The Hospital

Imagine white walls,
Sick people left to right,
Long, crowded, pale blue halls,
And being told
You can't go home that same night.

I thought I'd be left there
Forever and always.
A small pain became
A scary bridge to cross.
Nothing could ever be the same.

For the longest time,
I thought asthma might be the death of me.
It doesn't seem life threatening
To other people,
But I know what asthma feels like.
The strain on my lungs,
How it makes me wheeze at night,
How it makes my chest
Congested and tight,
That I had to use a machine to breathe.
It's never been something easy.
Yet people talk about it so casually.

Except, it wasn't asthma this time.
I was just a kid
And I had kidney problems.
My parents took turns being at the hospital.
I stayed at the hospital for a couple of weeks.
Maybe it was even longer.
It could've been as long as a month.
I don't remember.

All I know is I missed the first three weeks
Of the third grade and that bothered me.
I hated being behind everyone else.

The hospital was comfortable
Most of the time.
There was TV in the room.
The food was good and healthy.
My favorite part of the day was
The arts and crafts.
I made a bracelet out of beads
And drew pictures to color
The long, uncertain days
When I wasn't sure I'd get better.
Other family members visited
And my parents made sure
At least one of them was always there.
The hospital could never be home though,
Not if I stayed there for an entire year.

I'll never forget one thing
About that first night I was admitted.
A doctor made fun of my weight.
I don't remember exactly what he said
Or what his name was.
All I remember now is the fury
My mother brought upon him.
She made sure he was the one embarrassed.
She told the other doctors and reported him.
That was my mother.
That is my mother to this day.
She won't let anyone take advantage of her kids.
I just wish I'd never been sick at all.
I didn't choose to get sick,

But I wish I'd just been healthy enough
To never cause worry.
It must've been hard for my mom
To watch other kids get ready for school
While I was lying in a hospital bed.

## Closer Than A Role Model

You used to be
Someone I admired;
Almost like a role model.
You drank cappuccinos
And I thought it was cool
So I did that too.
I was too young to drink coffee.
I watched the same movies and shows
As you.
I let you put makeup on me.
I painted your nails and drew designs
On your feet.
It was always erasable art,
But you seemed to appreciate it.
I let you borrow movies.
You were what I esteemed to be,
Until I realized that every
Beautiful person has flaws inside them too.
My flaws are not a shame to hide.
They're what makes me who I am inside.

# Mama

My grandma had a sister.
We all called her Mama.
I can still remember her vaguely.
I didn't know her as well as
My parents or cousins did.
She liked Cadbury chocolates.
She had a pink floral nightgown.
She lived in the basement.
She seemed to have dealt with a lot,
To have been treated unfairly sometimes,
But she was always kind.
She used to have this walker for support
And her and my grandmother
Were so close.
They were the only two left
Out of all their siblings.
When Mama passed away,
It really affected everyone
Like a tremor,
Shaking up a lively city.
She's never been forgotten.
We visit her grave often
And leave flowers and chocolates.
It's nice when someone
Leaves such an impression
That their loved ones always
Pay their respects.
No one can tell how easily
They'll be forgotten
Or how long they'll be remembered.

# The Lost Garden

Where there is concrete
There was once a garden.
The front of my house
Wasn't always the dog's playpen.

We didn't always have a white fence.
The gate used to be gray and netted
By the narrow entrance.
The lock was always tough to open.
Yet, looking at it, I knew I was home.

The space still looks fine,
But when the garden was there
It seemed divine.

It feels like a lifetime ago,
That other animals used to pass
Where we planted seeds to sow
As I ran my toes through crisp grass.
Ladybugs would settle on the flowers.

We had soft blue hydrangeas,
Daisies, and pinecones
That the squirrels would devour.

A tall, strong tree
Stood over everything.
Whenever lightning struck
I always feared we'd run out of luck
And it would fall on the house,
Crushing all of us.
I thought the tree would always be there
And I pretended it was magical.
Even in fairytales,
Everything must have an end.

In the garden, the air felt fresher
And every once in a while I saw a rose.
All that beauty was destroyed
To create more space to roam.
Concrete replaced grass.
Time keeps moving so damn fast.
The tree trunk was cut into logs.
We wrapped Christmas lights around it
For a couple of years
Until it eventually disappeared
Like many relics from the past.

## Life Before Kindergarten

Reggae music playing;
Rotating, black disco ball,
Casting colorful lights.
Parties in the backyard,
With family and friends
For birthdays and just to celebrate.
Guyanese people sure know how to party.
Chicken curry made by grandma.
Trips to Canada to visit family,
Usually during the summer.
Swimming in the plastic pool outside.
I carefully walked in,
While my brother always ran
And plunged into the water fearlessly,
Never afraid or waiting on anyone.
Even back then,
I wished I could be more like that.
I was too shy, quiet, reserved;
Afraid of everything.
I thought anything
That could go wrong would.
I would never go up and just start talking
With anyone unless they invited me first.
Even then, I never felt like I belonged.
I did treasure life at home though.

*Chapter 2*

## School Days In Passing

SINCE I'M IN MY last semester of graduate studies, I felt it was important to look back at my academic life. I'm almost completely done with school and I realize it has taken up most of my life. It is a complete blessing to get to attend the schools I've graduated from. However, no kid loves school all the time and there are aspects of growing up that feel uncomfortable. I never had a lot of friends at school and it felt like no matter what I just never belonged there. My parents are from Guyana and I'm a first-generation immigrant. I never thought about how that affected the way I interacted with other people my age or how it brought about cultural clashes until I got older.

I really loved college and graduate school. I had the option of doing something I cared about and that is a blessing. I'm going to miss having a space to discuss social theories and current issues about race and gender. It seems like it's easy to talk about those things anywhere, but I've found that many of the jobs I've worked at were only interested in the work I could get done. It usually had nothing to do with human rights or actually discussing anything. I'm not afraid of doing a lot of work or multitasking. I like getting assignments done. There is a structure with school that I haven't found with certain jobs. There is a vague plan to follow. At school, there are many resources that make you feel secure and well guided through making tough decisions. Even if you make a mistake or fail at something, there is usually a way to correct it. We learn through trial by error. It becomes so much more difficult when you leave school and you no longer have that cushion of time to fall on for support. Adulthood, on the other hand, is messy, scary, and full of changes you never see coming. People can be cruel and they stop treating you kindly. The world doesn't seem as wide or exciting. It isn't full of opportunity as it was in younger years. The stress is not about picking a major or making your class schedule align or getting homework done. The new problems are out of control and they happen randomly. In fact, nothing seems to work out and you get frustrated, wondering when all the pieces of your life are supposed to come together?

Sometimes, I slow down my life and how I'm thinking because I'm afraid of moving forward too fast or what comes next. I definitely take time to process things, to reflect on memories, and to understand how I feel. I'm so nervous about my future and I thought that I'd understand life better once I was in my twenties. However, I still feel like I'm figuring out life and will be doing that for some time. Maybe most people my age and older feel that same way. That imposter syndrome never quite goes away does it? I've spent so much of my life in school that I'm worried I haven't had enough of a range of experiences. Looking back at the past and thinking about my journey through academics, specifically, has helped me understand I wouldn't change a thing. I love my life the way it happened and none of it was perfect, but it did all have a purpose. At first, school was this unpredictable space where sometimes I did very well and other times I couldn't seem to grasp the meaning of what we were learning. In early elementary school years, I did very well academically because I had a strong concentration on getting high grades. That is due in large to my mom. She would be working full time and then come home in the afternoon exhausted. She would just have time to have dinner and then she'd go right into helping my brother and I with our homework and with studying. She almost had no social life outside of going to work and then taking care of us. So, I have many people to thank for my education, but my mom is the one who really made it a priority for my brother and I to go to excellent schools and put effort into the work we were doing. Without her, there is no way I'd be motivated enough to complete a Masters Degree at the moment. My mom was an excellent student in Guyana and she had perfect grades. So, I always felt that pressure to do better and I knew from a young age that I should be aiming for college.

I struggled at times, but I think that is realistic and true of many students. Any type of failure or disappointment pushes you to try harder. I think high school is intentionally made difficult for almost everyone in order to prepare people for college and life after that as well. By the time you graduate, you realize you can handle the stress of being an adult because it feels much more natural and reassuring than high school years. Isn't it funny and sad how teenage years seem aimed at rebellion against childhood years? We don't allow ourselves to be childlike because we want to fit in. We want to be adults and then when we eventually hit adulthood, we want time to turn back. It wasn't until I graduated from high school that I realized how important it was to embrace my culture.

I'm not great at studying subjects I have no interest in, but when it comes to studying topics I'm passionate about, I can do very well. In life, there are always things that we don't want to do, but sometimes we have to do them either for people we care about or because it's part of growing up and being mature. It's also because we all have to be accountable for our actions, words, and deeds. School does teach you that. All those assignments I didn't want to do, all those tests that felt impossible, all the classes that felt pointless, had a purpose too. They showed me how to keep trying and that it does pay off one day.

## Kindergarten

Different and foreign;
A change I wasn't quite ready for.
Uncomfortable and boring;
Bad impressions created through lore.

School was a lore that my cousins told me
And I was so easily deceived.
They said I would no longer feel free.
I wish I could have believed
That everything would be okay,
But I knew the truth
Beyond what my parents would say.

The first day of school
Was the last day of a safer time.
Nothing about it seemed cool.
It didn't matter how much I whined.
I went to the first day of school,
But never made it into the building.
My aunt tried to drop me off.
That wasn't enough for the school.
They required my parents be there
Even though they were both working.
I should've seen even back then,
I wasn't going to fit in there.

## Kindergarten Graduation

It was my first real graduation
And I remember being nervous,
Excited, and confused.
I remember that even back then,
There weren't many people
For me to say goodbye to.
In the pictures,
I'm mostly alone.

I was wearing
A light blue dress.
We had a school play.
I thought it would be a big mess,
But it turned out more than okay.
It was performed before the graduation ceremony.
There were glistening lights
On the stage.
There was lots of blue
In the crafty costumes,
Which put me at ease.
I recall beautiful music and props
Like a big boat
And swirly waves
That we could all see.
Those little details
Helped me to believe
And escape into the scene.
We played out the story
Of Jonah and the big fish
That swallowed him
And kept him in its belly
For three days and three nights.
I don't think any of my graduations since

Have been so dramatic and stunning.
I was anxious and happy
That I graduated.
I knew it was an accomplishment
Even at that age.
Yet, the air was also filled
With a terrible sadness
For it was that same year
That a loved one had passed.
My family had gone
To that funeral
Not long before my graduation.
So strange how often
Celebration and mourning
Are equally mixed.

## Assumption

They take one look
At my brown skin.
They assume they know my religion.
They say they hear my words.
Then why do they ask me again?
They make us where the same shirts;
Still, they treat us different.

## Schoolyard Games

I hate playing jump rope
Because I always mess up the flow.
It's easier to watch
Then to participate and go.
Otherwise, I just botch everything up
And everyone laughs.
Sometimes it's fun,
Playing like that in the sun.
Other times, it's all a big dance.

Bright colored chalk for hopscotch,
Freshly painted on the pale sidewalk
As we hop down the squares.
Sometimes we do that in pairs,
As if it's a big accomplishment.
Running is not allowed,
Not even outside,
Because kids will get hurt.
So, instead, we skip
And just walk really fast.
Before the teacher can notice,
We're playing freeze tag.

# Halloween At School

I still think about
Kids telling scary stories
On Halloween,
Talking about trick-or-treating,
And all the classic Halloween movies
They were going to watch later at night.
We used to wear our costumes
At school and eat candy.
A kid in my class was dressed up
Like a vampire.
I remember a bunch of us
Were playing a game
Where he pretended to chase us.
It was so much fun,
But then he got in trouble
Because we were running too fast
And the teacher thought we would get hurt.
Another time,
I had a costume with spiderlike webs

And these two girls who were dressed like cats
Were chasing me,
Looking for string.
Only on Halloween,
Do you get to hang out with people
You'd never get to sit with at lunch.
My mom used to take off work early
And pick up my brother and I from school.
She always made sure
She could spend that time with us too,
No matter how hard she was working.
We'd go trick-or-treating
Around our neighborhood,
By the houses of family members,
And by Liberty Avenue.
I remember returning home
And my brother wouldn't eat any of the candy
Because he didn't have a sweet tooth like me.
Yet he loved to count each piece.
If he had more candy than me,
It made him feel like he had won a prize.

## Book Fair

Maybe it was the young writer in me,
But I used to love the book fairs
At school each year.
The teachers would hand out
A bunch of brochures
That showed us the books
That would be available for purchase.
I think we used to mark off
What we wanted
And our parents paid for it in advance.
Then we got the package
At school whenever it arrived.
It always felt special
And everyone in class
Wanted to know what you got.
I liked keeping the package closed
So that it would remain a mystery.

When we got older
And could bring our own money,
We didn't rely upon the brochures anymore.
We used to go to the actual book fair.
It was set up in the library
And it felt like another world.
It wasn't just books anymore.
You could buy fancy, fluffy pens,
Movie posters, keychains,
Colorful, bright trinkets,
And the books seemed more inviting
Than ever before.
I'd rather spend hours there
Than in my classroom anymore.

## What I Miss About Elementary School

Pizza Parties;
Is it sad that I miss pizza parties?
What about dress up days,
Watching movies
Every once in a while in class,
And feeling really safe?
I also miss celebrating Christmas in class,
Baking sweets and bringing them in
For my classmates to eat;
Exchanging gifts by pulling a name from a hat.
Yet, still, everyone puts special thought
Into the gifts they bought
For someone they hardly knew.

# Frizzy Hairs

I never knew what to do
With my frizzy hair.
My family would plait it.
I almost never wore it loose
In younger years at school
Because it was always getting knotted
And combing out knots
Hurt way more than I thought.
I don't know how I would
Always be losing strands
Of long, black hair
Everywhere I went
And yet, there was still so much
Thick black hair on my head.
Sometimes, my hair would be tied
Into a high ponytail,
With the hair looking extra puffy.
No matter how neatly tucked
My hair was,
These little frizzy hairs
Would stand up on my head.
I feel like people would stare.
They always find a way
To remind you that you don't belong.

To make it worse,
My crush used to make fun
Of my hair
And had this running joke
Of a pet named fluffy
Getting lost in my hair.
It was harmless humor
But also a reminder
Of not belonging there.

# Wish I Knew

In those days,
I knew nothing of social theory,
White privilege,
And Eurocentric beauty.
I didn't have the language
To identify what was wrong.
I couldn't explain why I felt less important,
Less noticed, less valued,
Less beautiful, and less eye-catching
Than the white girls in my class.
It's so easy to think you're the problem,
To feel like your culture
And appearance are what needs to be changed.
I wish I knew then
What I've learned since.

## Music Recital

I used to take band classes
And play the flute.
I remember this music recital.
I was so terrified
That I'd play the wrong note
And it would be very noticeable.
I should've worried more
About what I was wearing.
I had on this light blue,
Puffy, silk gown
With intricate little beads.
Everyone else was dressed
More simple and refined,
Wearing black and white outfits.
As I played the flute,
In the big auditorium,
I felt cold and jittery
Even though the site before me
Was bold and glittery;
A bright, beautiful sea
Of silver instruments
And music filling the space
With a sense of hope and care.
I forgot what I looked like
And thought only of the sounds
Erupting from the flute
And how the recital
Was not just about my music.
It was a wonderful symphony,
Where each person was a piece
Of a whole;

Creating rhythm and emotion,
Art and beauty
As we all learn to work together as well.

## Too Quiet?

All my life,
I've been told
I'm too quiet.
I just don't understand
How that bothers other people.
Why is the world so uncomfortable
With people who are quiet?
I'm not talking about absolute silence,
But sometimes less is more.
Sometimes, people need time
To process their thoughts,
To trust people,
To understand what they mean to say.
Otherwise, everyone
Would just blurt out
The first thing that pops into their mind.
At times,
That blunt honesty is helpful.
Some truths need to be said
And no amount of fine aging
Will make that harsh truth seem sweeter,
But sometimes letting thoughts
Marinate and allowing for some quiet
Gives words more depth.
I wish teachers, friends, family members,
Strangers in passing, and co-workers
Could've understood that concept more
Because I've always thought
Being quiet was a problem I needed to fix.

## The Year 2008

It was a year full of strife.
Betrayals hit me in the back
Like a knife.
A long state of winter
Devoured my world,
Spreading loss, deceit, and loneliness.
People I knew for years
Finally showed me their lowliness.

My grades were falling,
School was unbearable,
Long, tedious, and isolating.
It was my last year at that school,
But I couldn't wait to graduate.
It wasn't a bad place.
It always felt safe.
Yet, after nine years there,
I thought I'd feel more sentimental
About leaving it behind.
Instead, I just felt like it was time
To move on to better things.
High school would be a clean slate
And a much needed revival.
Most of my classmates were very respectful.
Though, there were enough faces
I wouldn't miss.

I didn't care about my birthday.
Even when I tried to celebrate it,
There was a massive blizzard outside.
I don't think it was the snow
That kept people away that year.

## Announcement

I wasn't close with anyone those days.
I would bring a book
To fill my time.
I read as much as I could,
While people chatted
In the morning before class.
One day at school,
There was an announcement
Regarding me.
I could feel the sting of death
Slowly approaching.
I could feel everyone staring.
I'd never felt less free.
The announcement said
That I would be absent
For the rest of the week.
My teacher was annoyed
As if it was my decision to miss school.
My classmates were gossiping.
No one asked me what I thought
Or how I felt.
They didn't care about the severity
Of what was really going on.
I barely ever cry in front of people,
But tears aren't the only sign of sadness.
Hearing that announcement
Felt like losing a battle.
I knew for a while that this big loss
Was coming for my whole family,
But knowing didn't make it any easier.

## Funeral In Canada

A funeral in Canada;
Death was in the air.
A frequent vacation spot,
Once a home away from home,
Became cold and vacant.

The fresh air in Canada
Felt tainted by this single event.
I couldn't cry,
But I was sad.
I was always shy,
But also mad.

I knew that so many people
I loved
Were sad and broken.
No words of comfort could be spoken.
Everything was a mess
And the hurt was felt deep in our family.
For awhile afterwards, my mom
Couldn't get good rest at night.
My grandmother was inconsolable.
The plug was pulled.
We knew this parting was coming,
But it wasn't a real goodbye.
The last time I saw him,
He was in terrible pain.
He could barely talk
As he lay uncomfortably in that hospital bed.
My mom lost her best friend.
Her brother since birth
Was no longer a part of this earth.

I wish I could've made her feel better,
But I could barely get through the eighth grade.
Ever since then,
Canada hasn't felt like a warm place.

# Recess

Recess;
An unpredictable space
With loud kids
And words without grace.
Fleeting actions,
Fleeting hurts,
Regrets;
Games that make no sense;
Not a place for silence.
No safety to rely on,
Not even from faces
Of those who seem like friends.

## Eighth Grade

The hours spent in recess
Were isolating.
It felt like an eternal winter.
I was confused the entire time.
It felt like an unlucky year
And my grades had never been worse than
They were that year.
I felt like everything I was doing
Was wrong, not enough.
I just didn't seem to fit in no matter
What I did.

# Two Worlds

School was uncomfortable.
In the later years,
I stumbled.
In the earlier years,
I did well academically.
My mom always pushed me
To do my best,
To not accept low grades.
I passed every single test.
I didn't understand back then
What my family went through
Just to be a part of this country
And I took it all for granted.

My mom was the best teacher.
No matter how high or low my grades were,
I barely had friends at school.
I didn't connect
With many of the students.
I was so quiet and many of them were loud.
I was too strange.
They never knew what I meant.
Was I too comfortable with being alone?
It's like the other kids just alienated me
Or noticed I was different.

I wish the two worlds could've mixed better,
That I'd have felt more comfortable
Bringing up things that I liked,
Regarding my culture and my family,
At school.

## High School Freshman

Freshman year
And I'm already off
To a bad start.
People moved so fast,
Day by day,
Without a care.
I felt panic rise in my heart.
Everything became much more
Revolved around technology
And I felt pressure to keep up
With this intense race
That high school encouraged.

Screens in classrooms
And homework piled high
Always enforced gloom
And made me open my books
With a sigh.
So many classes;
My eyes were still adjusting
To just wearing glasses
And taking the train and bus home.
A different class schedule
Each day of the week
Made me shake my head and moan.
I feel like I never got used
To that constant change
And the speed of that pace.
I was always taking my time
And if there's one thing I learned
From freshman year
It's that time was never mine.

## Fire In The Attic

I remember walking down the hill
Most afternoons.
My bag was breaking one day,
Tearing away by the seams
Much like my motivation.
I remember struggling
To swipe the metro card
When it was still new to me
And feeling like everything was too hard.
It was all moving too fast
And I was barely catching my breath
From all the stress.

I remember watching *Paranormal Activity*
In theaters with friends
Sometime in October.
A week later,
A fire in my attic felt like the end.
I'm sure there was no connection.
Thank goodness it was only
That one section
Of our entire house.
Otherwise, I'm not sure
What we would've done.

We couldn't stay in the house
For a long while
Because the damage was severe enough
To warrant many repairs.
I didn't think about it at the time
Though it must've been hard
For my parents to deal with.
Our house wasn't burned to the ground.
Still, it's a big adjustment to make
When my parents also came from another country
And spent years saving up
To actually invest in a house.
They had to start over yet again
In a different way.

My dad had lost his job at the time
And he had to do mostly freelance work.
My mom was still working in the city,
But the new house
We moved into temporarily
Was also further away
From the subway station.
Coming home from work
At night in the freezing cold
Must've been tedious and rough.
That winter was very tough,
Where we didn't have
The familiar comforts of our home,
But we made do with the resources
That we did have.
Most importantly,
We were all safe and healthy.

## Subway Rides

A man singing about fried chicken;
A woman eating jello with a metro card;
You never know what you're going to get.
Every train ride is a gamble.
Some people cause eyebrows to raise
With the way they ramble,
Ready to argue
Or push and shove you.
Never mind how crowded
The train or the bus are;
There is never enough space.
People pile in
Like it's a game of sardines.
Train delays;
Long, rainy days
Where the bus takes forever
And you don't feel like walking home
Because the umbrella is about to break;

Even when you get home
Time has simply
Slipped away.

## Yearbook Of Memories

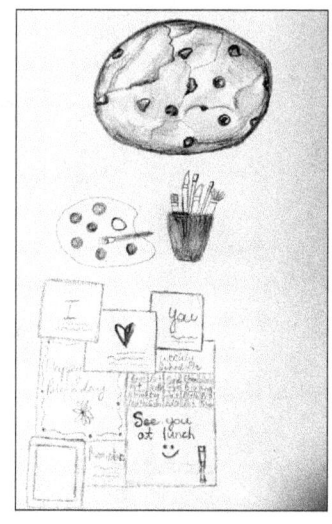

Locker surprises on birthdays,
Photographs to decorate
A cluttered space,
And caring notes
That people prefer to write
Than to say;
Having half days at school,
Wearing a uniform,
And not having to worry
About picking out outfits
Each morning in a hurry;
Walking to the art cottage,
Reading magazines in the library
During free time,
Worrying about all the exams,
And eating that moist, large chocolate chip cookie
With friends in the morning;

Doing lab experiments in science class,
Looking at beautiful artwork
In the hallways,
Gazing upon that castle-like building,
Running up that hill
In gym class,
Knowing that I'll see
The same faces each day,
And making a yearbook of memories
As time passes.

## Gratitude For Parents

I am more grateful
Than words can abide.
These four years of growth
Have been one crazy ride!

Though I struggled to know
How to be a teenager,
I survived high school
All the same
And never got into much danger.
When I graduated,
It was a celebration,
Not just of my efforts.
More importantly, it was appreciation.

I have many people to thank.
Yet, it starts with two people
Who are the highest in the ranks.
They provided shelter, love,
Safety, comfort, and a happiness
That was more than enough.
Thank you to my mom
For continually pushing me to be better,
For not accepting failures,
For providing wise words
That no one else could say better,
For being both friend and mother,
And for being a great role model.
She joined me on adventures
Where we traveled the world.
We still watch our favorite shows
And movies together.
It always makes me feel safe

And less alone.
The warmth of her love
Could never be paler
Than the brightest red rose,
Nor her courage and strength
Less durable and tough
Than iron shields and steel swords.

Thanks to my dad
For driving me to school in the mornings,
For following a carpool schedule
And committing to that,
For taking my brother and I
To the doctor
Every time we were sick,
For picking us up from school
Whenever we needed it,
For teaching us how to swim
And ride a bike in the backyard,
For providing any resource
I needed
Whether it was a new phone,
A computer or a greater resource still
In freedom, love, and acceptance.

My parents both grew up in Guyana
And they had strict childhoods
And less of the opportunities
I was given so easily.
Yet, they never restricted
My brother or I
And instead treated us the same,
Never taking sides.
They pushed us to take responsibility

For our words and actions
And to keep working hard
On our dreams and ambitions.
I can never repay
The true value of what was given.
All I can do is say
That I'm thankful for this love
And wish it to never be ridden.

## High School Years

I remember high school too well.
It was mixed with excitement
And disappointment.
There were great adventures
And solid friendships.
I remember finding solace through art,
Getting lost in what I'd start
But rarely ever finish.
Progress reports
Were the emblems of my failure.
I felt guilt after report cards,
Parent-teacher conferences,
And knowing how my mom
Struggled to pay tuition all the while.
She labored at a job for years
Just so my brother and I
Could have a good education.
I don't think I tried hard enough.
I could've done better
And back then,
I was neglectful.
I needed to be faster, smarter,
A multi-tasker.
Instead, I felt like a failure.
No matter how fast I moved,
It was still too slow.

I graduated on time.
I never actually failed a class.
Still, I had trouble with consistency.
Now those years are gone.
The good thing is that
The overwhelming feeling

Of not being enough
Pushed me to try harder in college.
Without the losses, failures,
And rejections of the past,
The victories,
The successes,
And joys of the future
Would not have been possible.

# Purchase Road

A bus often called the loop
By students;
A long, winding road
That many embark upon;
A tree that may as well
Have been in a horror movie;
Woods that stretch on
And fade into the fog;
Gloomy weather from night till dawn;
Mist spreading over campus.

Wandering around Westchester,
Restlessly searching for adventure
Or just something to do;
Going to the mall
And eating total junk food;
Calories piling in a semester
Like tuition bills, loans,

And doubts about majors and careers.
Things that seem far off in a land of worry
 Still cause stress in freshman year of college.
The sites at Mamaroneck Avenue
Are less crowded than a city I miss.
They're more intimate and local,
But it still fails to feel like home.
Shopping for fall clothing
To escape from the dreariness
Of daily routines
And unsettling uncertainty;
I miss those days
When it was so easy to find
What I wanted to wear.
It didn't feel like a chore
Or a tiresome bore.
Binge watching *American Horror Story*
And ordering veggie dumplings;
Finding solace with friends at a movie theater
Or at a play performance;
Working out at the gym
To take the edge off of not knowing
Where I'm headed.

## Library Cages

Library cages;
I never checked out a single book.
I barely got work done.
Not enough spaces;
The library was a strange spot,
But I visited that space a lot.
I don't know why.
Too many pages
And not enough action;
Yet, it felt more calming
Than all the other corners of campus
Besides my dorm.
The basement of the library
Didn't feel like a basement at all.
It was large and comfortable;
A place to socialize.
Lips locked of different ages
And I don't know what the rage is.
Building of blue glass,
Green sofas inside;
We lock ourselves in study,
Force the focus,
But my mind wanders;
I keep getting lost.

## The Stood

Dark of night,
Smoke blowing in the air;
Some of it is mysterious fog;
Most of it comes
From students' mouths.
They draw cigarettes from their lips,
Backs against the building,
They're escaping and relaxing.
Is this adulthood yet?
When does the real fun start?
The stood is a place on campus,
But it feels miles away
In another world of mischief.
Bands play there,
But the music is so loud
I can barely hear or speak.
The couches are old and overused.
The pool tables are too crowded.
There's art hanging in every room;
Hardly any gratitude.
We cross the main road,
Wet with rain,
Deserted and open.
We climb the stairs up to the stood
And people have their drinks
In brown paper bags outside.
Why is getting drunk so enticing
For college students, for adults?
Every time I visit the stood
It's always a different mood,
But I never settle into the space.
Moments fleet so fast,
Spinning, fading, aging.

Culture shock, zombie prom, speed dating.
One year I'm there;
The next I'm gone.

## What Do I Say?

What can I contribute
That someone else hasn't already said?
I feel the need to speak,
To push out smart words,
But my brain is freezing.
It's glitching like a slow computer.
How do I express my feelings?

That is no excuse,
But I can't stop hesitating,
Overthinking, guilt tripping
For being so silent.
I hate doing so much reading for class
And then not knowing what to say
In class discussions.
So I keep quiet but have so much to express.
I never want to disrupt the flow.
I have a lot to add and I agree
With what people are saying.

I'm proud of who I am.
I feel confident in my opinions.
I can be so outspoken that
People don't want to listen
Or deal with my passion.
Yet, there are many moments in time
When I'm quiet and hesitant.
I won't just come out and state my reactions
To readings and critical theories,
To social issues and histories.

Sometimes I really want to say something.
I just don't know what to say.

Sometimes I'm not that interested
Or I don't fully understand
Or I simply want to listen
And absorb the thoughts before I comment.
Time passes and I never speak
And the class ends.
My chance is gone.
I missed the social conversation.

I want to participate.
I don't know how to do that
In a way that feels natural
Where my words are eloquent,
Where my points are strong and worth hearing.
Sometimes I want to be a part
Of something
So badly,
But I find myself just listening,
Waiting, and admiring the conversation.
When do I jump in?

## Changes In College

I think about college
And immediately picture
Changing environments,
Changing friendships,
Different versions of myself
Shifting, evolving,
Unexpectedly growing,
Harnessing strength, and knowledge.
Every year,
I learned something new
About myself
Because one year
I was dorming upstate
And the next I moved back home and was
Commuting to a local school.
I didn't miss a beat.
I adapted so quickly
Because I'm terrified of change
And yet I deal with it well enough.

I guess no one knows
Where they will end up
Until they take a chance and go.
Life shouldn't be stifled.
It shouldn't feel static or recycled
Of old mistakes
That are spinning like a wheel.

# What Comes Next

School was a big part
Of my identity.
Sometimes I loved school.
Sometimes I was exhausted by it.
It feels like school
Has always been there
For most of my life;
Almost two decades of school.
It's a safety net,
But I can't be too safe with my decisions
Going forward anymore.
It's okay to make mistakes,
To feel like everything is brand new,
Strange, and uncomfortable.
As I finish my last semester
Of grad school,
I'm terrified
But also intrigued
For what comes next.

## Writing With I

Using the word I
In writing for school
Is often deemed
Too personal.
I recall being instructed
Many times
To discard of I
Because it doesn't seem professional.
It's considered too informal
And yet it's the most normal
Way of speaking.

I've read essays
Where critics condemn
Emotional writers
Who use I in their works.
Heaven forbid
That a writer gets too emotional,
Especially if that writer
Is a woman.
Well, why would anyone
Want to read writing
That is unemotional and vacant?
Why is emotion such a negative
To begin with?
In academia,
In writing, in ruling,
In many careers,
I is unwanted
And too personal to matter.
It's as if we're too taunted
By emotion and feeling.
We prefer mindless chatter

And need to be robots in writing
To prove we're detached enough
To be taken seriously.

## English As A Major

Choosing a major in college
Was always difficult for me.
Some people know what they want to do
Since they're children
Or some are influenced by their parents' dreams.
Some people don't even get to choose a major.
Their futures are already mapped out for them.
They're expected to follow that plan
And whatever they study in college
Is just a means to an end.

I had choices and time to decide
And I kept changing my mind
And growing frustrated with myself for not knowing.
When I finally picked English as a major,
Pieces of my life fell into place.
I still had no idea what my specific career would be,
But the experience of taking English classes
Helped me become who I am.
I found my voice
Through reading other people's strong words
And listening to voices that were unwavering
In their beliefs.
I saw the social issues of the world more clearly.
I found greater respect for the tedious process of writing.
It's not just about telling stories
Or escaping through art,
But art itself is a reflection of the world we live in.

It felt like finally there was a place
Where I belonged and really thrived.
It took great work and dedication,
More than people would imagine,

To be an English major;
To dedicate your time
To not just reading books,
But making arguments
Like an attorney
Or close reading, analyzing, and researching
Like an investigator or a doctor in the lab.
There is depth in every class
And every year
Demanded more growth from me.
I was challenged and I felt fulfilled.
Little did I know,
That the journey was only beginning.

There are always going to be doubts
When you take risks
And tread down a path few people you know
Have gone down before.
I don't think many other members of my family
Majored in English or took the creative path.
My parents were supportive of what I wanted to do,
But I know there have always been concerns too
Of how I'm going to make a living
And whether I made the right choice?

Well, nothing in life is guaranteed.
No job is completely secure
And while some jobs do have a greater likelihood
Of financial stability than others,
Money shouldn't be my sole drive in life.
My mom always says
"You don't how hard life is out there."
I used to feel like she was underestimating me,
But she was only trying to prepare me.

She is right.
I have no idea what it's like to come to another country
Like she did and start over,
Have the degree I achieved mean almost nothing
In that new country,
And work jobs that I am overqualified for
If only to provide for my family.

I have the choice to choose what I want to do
Because my parents sacrificed their own dreams.
They worked jobs to make money for their families
And I don't take that fact lightly.
I understand a lot is expected of me
And I judge myself and my choices
More critically than most.
I chose English as a major
Because I wanted more out of my life
Than working at jobs
Where I have no say,
Where I'm only a source of labor,
Where my words and thoughts don't matter,
And where I feel my passion for life
Dies day by day.
Of course, if I had to choose between my dreams
And taking care of the people I love
By settling into dull jobs that will provide for them,
I'd still choose the people I love always.

I'm proud of this chapter in my life,
Of being an English major,
And I'm making my peace with it coming to an end.
I hope it's not completely the end though.

I hope I can find those jobs
That let me bring in the knowledge
I've acquired
And also help me provide for the people
I care about.
Contrary to what most people in the world believe,
English is not an unnecessary major
By any means.
It has great value and meaning.
It can teach you more about yourself,
How you fit into this world,
And what you can contribute to this world
More than most majors
That are credited with giving
The tools for success.

## Chapter 3

## Artist In Progress

I THINK OF ART as meaning more than just drawings, paintings, and sketches. Art is a work of creation that someone puts emotion and energy into. Music is art. Writing is art. Baking is art. Photographs are art. It still amazes me how a photograph can capture the energy and feeling of a moment in time. Photographs preserve your memory of someone you loved. I like taking photographs for that reason and because it also reminds me of drawing and painting. Playing with filters and lighting is much like rendering colors in a drawing or painting. I believe that art comes in many forms and each one has the capacity to help people understand themselves and the world they live in.

I feel like people always misinterpret me. I was a quiet kid. Then, I was a quiet teenager. At times, I'm still a quiet adult. Slowly, I've found my voice. I still feel comfortable with sometimes being quiet because I don't feel the need to say something unless I mean it. When I was younger, I felt like it was a bad thing to be quiet in school because in school, being quiet was viewed as something that needed to be fixed. Teachers always tried to get quiet students to participate even if they weren't comfortable doing so. They kept emphasizing the importance of "breaking out of our shells." However, even when I break out of my shell, I still retreat back there sometimes. I could contribute good ideas in a group project or answer a question in class, but that doesn't mean I'll always be ready to be loud and speak my mind. I'm quiet if I need time to think about my opinions and school should be an environment that encourages students to think even if that means think quietly at times. I remember how easily students that raised their hands first in class were shown favoritism or if they were simply talkative, they were regarded as special. The more deep that my thoughts are, the more quiet I become. I'm quiet when I'm processing something slowly. I'm quiet when I'm uncomfortable and I'm getting to meet someone for the first time. Quiet isn't always a bad thing. It just means someone is feeling the full weight of a situation before they can take action or share how they feel.

Because I was so quiet, drawing artwork was my favorite way of communicating for awhile. Art has always been an area of interest for me since I was a kid and I found comfort in coloring inside coloring books and trying to capture detail in drawings. I never dreamed that I would show any skill in it until the summer after I graduated from the eighth grade. I bought a sketchbook, but rarely used it. One day, I looked at a picture of a tiger and pushed myself to capture as much detail as I could. I spent hours drawing it and by the end, I was impressed by how closely it matched. A few months later, I began high school and took a studio art class there. Our first big assignment was to do a drawing of eyes and render it in colored pencil. I drew a cheetah with blue eyes. It was the beginning of a long creative journey for me. I've kept drawing throughout different periods of my life because there is something soothing about drawing, coloring, using pastels, and painting. I'm taking anything that causes frustration or anxiety and I am physicalizing it in a drawing. It makes me feel better instantly. I can be in a good mood and want to draw also. The point is that it really expresses how I feel better than words can. It's important to have space to do that. I never tried to turn my love for drawing into a career because I didn't think people would invest in my drawings. There are also so many incredible career paths for people that draw and many talented people already in those roles that I didn't think it was necessary for me to venture off in that direction too. I just wanted to keep my drawings something deeply personal and special to me. When I draw, I draw because it genuinely makes me happy.

Writing is another thing I have passion for and it's more than a hobby as well. I see it as my potential career path. The career section of my life has always been a very ambiguous, frustrating, and stressful section. I get mad at myself sometimes for not having clearer plans about my future and what I'm aiming for. All throughout my childhood, I kept changing my mind about what I wanted to be when I grew up. I wanted to be everything from a hairstylist, a chef, a psychologist, a fashion designer, a screenwriter…etc. The list keeps going on. I've thought about teaching and working in the publishing industry because I was an English major. I want to keep what I studied in school with me as I move ahead in life. I want to be a writer, but the world makes me feel like this profession is not a valid career path sometimes.

My art style is too messy. My writing style is too truthful and intense. I feel like people don't want me in all my depth. They don't want to see me or to hear me in my whole range. They want me toned down, filtered, and blemish free. In the past few years, I've grown the most as an artist. I'm still growing and learning. One of the most important lessons that I learned is that validation from others shouldn't be the main goal in creating art. Draw, write, create because it means something special to you. There is absolutely no guarantee that what you create will pay your bills, be accepted by other people, be published, be chosen just like there is no guarantee that your creations will be failures, will receive backlash and criticism, will mean nothing to no one. The act of starting to create something should come from your heart. Let it begin there and as your creation grows, just keep remembering that you are creating something for you. It's a wonderful feeling when other people support you and show love for what you've created. However, your creativity is not just a tool through which to receive attention and flattery from people. Honor it by doing what feels right and letting yourself feel that contentment that comes with completing a piece of artwork or a story or a poem. It takes a whole journey to get there and it's very easy to tear that apart and forget that in mere minutes.

## Wanderer

I don't know what I'm searching for.
All I know is I keep wanting more.
I lose people left to right.
Most of them
Don't even put up a good fight.
They let go like they never cared.
It makes me wish I had never shared.

Sometimes, I'm drained.
I still don't want to rest
Or accept defeat.
I need to take care of myself.
I need to breathe and sleep.
Even in my dreams,
I keep wandering,
Searching for something.

I don't know what it is yet.
Maybe that is why I like creating art.
It's an adventure without regrets.

## Never Enough

No matter what I do it's never enough.
Does anyone feel that way too?
Spending years working on a degree,
Borrowing loans,
Working jobs that feel constraining,
Dealing with unnecessary drama;
Feels like it's always raining.

For every minute of joy and victory,
There's also failure and misery.
Taking so much time to create
And being judged and deconstructed
In mere minutes by hate;
It makes me want to give up sometimes
Before I've really even taken a great risk.

I spend so much time talking
About how I want to be a writer,
But I only recently started finishing
The stories I began years ago.
Even with gratitude and contentment
For each publication,
I always feel I'm moving too slow.

## Saturday Stress

Stacks of paper are piled
On this bed I've turned into a desk.
Scribbled old notes,
Bright yellow highlight marks;
It's all a mess.

Right beside the paper,
On top of a mountain of books,
Is an empty coffee cup,
Wearing a hot pink lip stain.
Art supplies are scattered recklessly
On purple sheets.
It's a reminder that pastel chalk
Still heals my pain.
Lately, I've been feeling strange.
Everything seems to be a game.
I'm cold, confused, and lonely,
Except when I'm creating art.
I never know where to start,
But listening to how I feel
Is enough to make it through the day.

I turn on the news
And it all seems like lies
Or some twisted truth;
Not the reality
I wanted to be a part of.
I still believe that a woman
Can be whoever she wants to be,
Even if the world continues to cater
To the male gaze.

The phone is vibrating with texts,
Pointless notifications, and reminders
When all I want to do is rest.
My foot keeps shaking as it hangs off the bed.
My mind rattles with thoughts unsaid.
One moment people are alive,
The next they're dead.
In one stage of life you're surrounded by friends,
The next, you're alone and the world is ending.
Why does life keep changing?
Why do I take forever to adjust?

There's one day left before morning traffic
Hammers into my ears.
It's so much like the buzzing of bees.
Tension and stress seep into my life
Long before I make it to work most days.
The moment the phone rings at my desk,
Panic rises in my chest.
People call only to yell
And if I were to yell back,
They'd call me crazy.

My favorite sound is either the coffee machine
Pouring another cup of coffee at home
Or when I can hear the rain dancing on the pavement.
Saturdays are supposed to be fun.
Instead, I've got a million tasks to do in one day
And I can never get any of it done.

## Let It Go

I can't let it go.
First I need to confront it.
I need to make a fight,
An explosion of emotion,
To express myself truly.
I can't let go of the past
Until it's actually acknowledged.
Most of the people around me
Rarely want to be honest about
Their own faults.

## Sad

I'm a happy person,
But right now I feel sad.
I want to keep creating,
But every word written
Makes me feel frustrated and mad.
A library of masterpieces haunts me;
Authors who perfectly captivated
How I am feeling but can never truly express.
Can the joy of making something stop the hating
By those who are too weak and miserable to try?
Too much regret and unjustified taking;
My doubts silhouette
And my head is aching.
It's making the glory I achieve
Feel so small.
Still, there's an undeniable beauty in the ordinary.
Even if my success is short lived,
If no one buys my books or listens to my words,
At least I dared to be an active part of this world
Even when other people tried to force me to retreat.
So much hesitation and determination;
I'm tired of feeling like a doormat
At work and in relationships.
Is this a case of imposter syndrome
Or is it something that will never end?
This lonely, despairing feeling of dissatisfaction;
Is it too much thinking
Or lack of action,
Or is it just a passing
Cloud of sadness?

## Words and Power

You're at your best,
Focusing on your good qualities.
You're at your best,
Improving yourself,
Improving this world,
Supporting, understanding,
And helping people.

You're at your worst
When you're picking people apart;
Can't stay focused on your work;
You don't even know where to start
Because you're too busy
Thinking of who has wronged you.

Words are special.
Words are power.
Don't ever let the anger devour
Your words, your truth turned sour.

## Tough Skin

I've heard too many people say
"You've got to have tough skin."
At work, at home,
The motto is still the same.
It makes me feel alone.
Tough skin means getting past emotions
And keeping a steady mind;
Means not breaking under pressure,
Nor letting old wounds unwind.

Don't post this and don't post that!
Social media is a terrible trap.
It's not the place to be so open about your feelings.
Go to therapy otherwise you're not really dealing
With pain or trauma or words unsaid.
Keep your feelings buried deep inside,
Like a history of guilt
Based on shameless pride.
Keep it buried deep like the sea,
Where bodies sunk beneath the water,
And human stories that mattered
Were left a mystery.

## For Women Of Color

You are not an exotic beauty
For a white man to notice or claim,
Nor unattractive or too simple-minded
To understand politics
That keep you contained
In lower levels of a social hierarchy
Built from greed, blood, and insecurity.
You do not need to be corrected
By white people
If your English doesn't sound proper enough.
Your accent is beautiful and special;
A marker of your culture and heritage.
Your language matters
Even if some people don't understand it.
It's not always your job to explain.
You are not a problem
For a white woman to diagnose.

They love your culture
Only when it benefits them;
Traveling to paradise locations
Without talking with the locals
Or caring about the struggles
Of the people that live there.
They love eating spicy foods
And learning about the dazzling aspects
Of your culture,
But they disregard the hardships.
They don't really want to hear about your problems.
About the struggles you face
With men in your own culture at times,
Or the sacrifices you make for loved ones,
Or the lack of options you have compared to them.

It reminds them of their privilege
And then they have to feel guilt
And they prefer to avoid that at all costs.
The more that you preach,
The more they call you names
Like petty, ungrateful, and rude.
They try their best to deduce
Your striking voice
As if to say you're only "complaining" and "oversharing."
Just know that they can't overpower you;
Not you in all your brilliance, range, and complexity.
You are so much more
Than the world has written for you.

You are not a voice lost in the margins
Of a classic story in the canon
That is also deeply flawed upon second look.
You are not a minor character
In a film about white people
Made for white people
In an industry controlled by white people.
Your words of conviction and truth
Should not be so easily dismissed
Like a fleeting gust of wind
Or a strong wave that breaks on the shore.
You move forward,
You keep growing,
But you should know your life matters;
Your words that take up space
And put dents in their
Polished, self-serving views
Do in fact matter!
Those feelings should be released.
Don't wait for people to agree.

Don't count on them being decent
And meeting you halfway.
Change is coming with every bold action,
Every ounce of hope, and respect for each other.
Some people still want everything their way.
They will never stop making you work
To be a part of their lives,
To feel included,
To make you believe that only you are the problem,
Never them.
Resist it,
Fight for yourself, your values,
And those you love.
Believe in yourself and all that you've worked for
And don't let anyone,
Even if they're people that claim to care,
Treat you like less than you are.

## Art Takes Time

I've been told
Art takes time.
I guess that is fine.
I keep creating,
Keep searching,
Keep hoping, and keep failing.
All the while I'm fighting,
Struggling, and breaking
Until I find something that is mine.

Some artists are perfectionists
But not me.
My style of art and writing
Is messy and free.
My proportions in drawings
Aren't always accurate.
I don't blend pastels perfectly
Because I like
When the color pops brightly.
I don't hold my pen steady.
My writing can feel heavy.

It won't be long now.
I'll get to show the world
What I made somehow.
I won't fade away
Like all the half-baked thoughts
That never got written down
Or the artists whose names
Are rarely found.

## Is That A Valid Career?

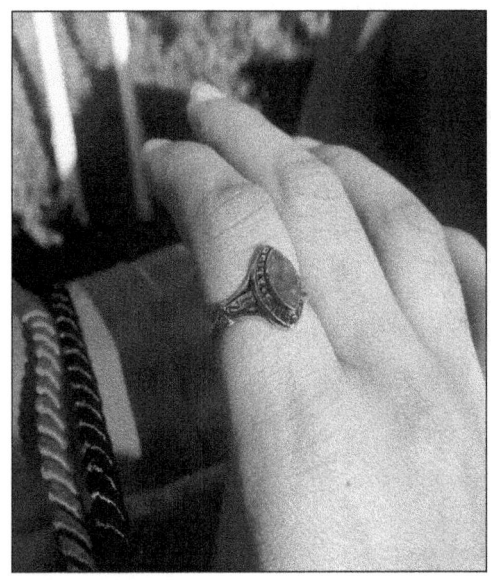

Writing isn't a profession.
That is how it feels
Or how the world makes you feel
When you're asked
"What jobs are you aiming for?"
You say with nervous tone,
"I want to be a writer."
Most people are nice.
They smile and nod
And don't say anything more.
Some people hint
"That's very competitive."
Family members or strangers,
Everyone usually has an opinion
About how successful you'll be.
Few actually listen to what you're saying.

## Golden Times

Fame, fortune,
Attention, and speculation;
Dreams do come true
And then some parts of you die.
People plaster their opinions
As fast as you write songs.

You move to the rhythm,
Never missing a beat.
You keep us alive
And we keep trying
To set you on fire
With shame and desire.
Give us your best, love.
We'll show you your worst.

Spotlight on your soul
And the world won't let you be;
We think we've claimed you
From childhood to when you're old.
We blast off comments like relatives
Who are disappointed
You're not doing what you were told.
Nothing is good enough,
Not your talent, your platform, your kind deeds;
Certainly not all the cracks in your beauty:
Flaws, cries for help, and misdemeanors.
The internet is a record
Of everything you've done wrong,
But what about everything you've done right?

What about all the times
That you got back up
And kept trying
No matter how often
Failure consumed your thoughts?
You're an artist, a ball of raw emotion.
Yet, you're not allowed to be human.
It's sad to witness a soul,
Once vibrant and evergreen,
That has dried out
From being in the sun too long.

## Untouchable

Quiet, reserved,
Almost other worldly;
Icon, legend, symbol,
But are they relatable?
Or has the success
Made it impossible
To find the humanity within?
"Their personality seems dry,"
Is what other people say.
Don't ask me why.
I see how hard some people try,
Never quitting, never surrendering
To the criticism they receive.
The more quiet you are,
The more mysterious you seem.
We judge people so quickly
And we only respect them
When they're gone.

## Lasting Relics

I always think things are worse
Than they actually are.
I don't know why that is.
I anticipate failure and struggle
As if it's my fate to fall.
I've got so much potential inside me.
I've got so many people who love me.
For that reason,
I think I ought to slow down the pace
Because it's not about the race
Or destination.
Your purpose can't be calculated
Solely by material success.
It's the appreciation of each day
I am alive
That pushes me to keep trying.

I should take a moment to be grateful
And stop feeling the hate.
I have talent and skill
And years of education
That helped me build up my confidence.
I have memories of love and friendship.
I've been protected and defended.
If I look forward to more sunshine and bright days
Maybe I'll stop feeling stuck
Or lost in doubt.

## Work It Out

Work on it,
Rehearse, and practice.
Don't aim for perfection.
It doesn't exist.
Make a more realistic list
And set your goals high
But not so much
That you set yourself up for failure.
Even if you fall short,
At least you tried.
Keep working
Pushing the limit till you make it.

## Balance

Where there is peace,
There is also silence;
A knowing that you're right
Where you're supposed to be
For now, anyways.
Change never ends,
But we endure with it don't we?
Growing and breaking,
Learning as we fail,
And failing so we can keep learning;
Where I once was whole,
My life rests in two halves.
These two worlds
Are divided each day
And I try to keep it all separate.
For, should they merge,
Should they leak
With chaotic beauty,
What monstrosity would I become?
If I stop trying to keep it all separate,
Let it combine and evolve,
What would I see before me?
For the world
Is not one thing or the other.
It's all in shades that you find the middle
And there is where I'll dwell.

*Chapter 4*

# Parting Is All We Know

I HESITATED BEFORE WRITING some of these poems and other parts just came fizzling up to the surface because there were so many words that never got said. This section is difficult and frustrating for me to write and let the world see. It's deeply personal and sad at times. I explore feeling as hopeless as when life dies around me and I'm not sure if it's ever going to grow back. This is also a section where I found I had the most to say because many feelings were bottled up to spare other people's feelings. I didn't want to dwell on feelings of anger, despair, frustration, loss, and separation because I know there are so many things to feel grateful about in my life. There are struggles and social issues that deserve more attention right now and I think everyone deals with things in their own way. It's hard to tell what someone is really feeling when they don't share that with you. It's also hard to be able to share feelings you don't fully understand right away. What I learned from school and the social climate of our world right now most of all is that something can feel uncomfortable and wrong, but you may not be able to identify what it is until you're older and understand more about social conditioning, injustices, cultural clashes, and social theory. Until I picked up more language that described how uncomfortable I felt, until I read social narratives penned by women of color for women of color, I didn't know how to communicate my discomfort. I didn't even think it was worth saying because growing up, whiteness was glorified and it still is. When white girls or white women talk about their lives or complain about issues they're facing, it's usually taken seriously. When women of color or girls of color do the same thing, it's inconvenient and we're told that our problems are problems we need to deal with.

My mind is never just stuck on bad things or negative feelings. I'm usually much more positive and optimistic than most people can handle. However, I get sad just like anyone else and feel upset about things I can't control. I get disappointed by relationships I thought I knew, but proved to be emptier than a tree without leaves. It didn't seem fair to just focus on the positive aspects of my life and the warmth of connections, places, memories, and experiences. The sad moments are just as important.

Partings are never easy and yet they happen at many points in life. It can be as simple and expected as graduating from school and leaving behind that academic part of your life. It can be as natural and still frustrating as parting from childhood years and growing up. It's always scary, unpredictable, and brings change into your life. People part ways in romantic relationships, family relationships, and friendships because people change. Sometimes, there are conflicts or some connections just fade away. However, it's important to realize those relationships fade because people let them fade. We all have a responsibility in a relationship and it's easy to avoid someone or to leave without confrontation. It's harder and more uncomfortable to speak out loud what you feel and to actually say goodbye. Goodbyes with people we love, with places we treasure, and with who we used to be are terrifying. Perhaps, that is why some partings happen without a goodbye. Some partings don't require words or some people are too afraid to say those words.

The year 2020 has been ripe with partings. I observed how the year began with death even before the Corona cases rose in New York. I went to three funerals for people who had deaths that were unrelated to the virus. I've seen partings quake through life and leave wreckage and open wounds for too many souls. I've heard cries of anguish for loved ones who are never opening their eyes to the world again. Death is so natural and yet it feels wrong every time it strikes. We don't ever get over losing a loved one. I think that emotional wound is always there. What is remarkable and a true show of strength is how we move forward even with the pain of the past and the weight of a terrible loss. We adjust our lives, adapt to the changes, find new reasons to live, and we honor the ones we lost by appreciating every day we get the opportunity to live.

## Upon A Dream, Once

Roses amongst thorns,
Castles built from bliss,
Partings meant to mourn
People we don't want to miss.
Jewel-like memories
Made to adorn
Are now deeply embedded
In the frost and are forlorn.

I thought I knew you,
Upon a dream, once.
I knew who you were
Because you were me;
Naïve, hopeful, and becoming.

Lost in dreams,
Faces keep changing,
But nothing is ever as it seems.
When you're losing people left to right,
It's hard to distinguish
What's wrong and what's right.
When you get older
And keep crossing lines,
Keep breaking rules,
Keep fighting systems
That are much too cruel,
Biased, and one-sided,
Your words of conviction
Appear to the world misguided.
You lose all connection
To the warmth of younger years.
Adulthood seems gray;
A perfect daydream
Gone to waste.

Isolated and stifled;
Relationships shift like clay,
Unmolding from specific shape.
You can't take back the words
You wish you didn't say.
It's the same way you can't bring back
The moment to speak
What was repressed.
Is it all a dream
Or some nightmare that we made?

# Ghost

I want to move on.
Shouldn't there be a light?
How do I know what to look for
When I've lost all reason to fight?
I remain forever in-between and stuck,
Searching for a truth that doesn't exist.
I don't fear death
For it happens day by day.
I fear being trapped,
Getting lost, and thrown away.
What if death occurs
And there is no moving on?
What if I walk the earth restlessly
And no one cares that I'm gone?

# Raw

Raw, unspoken,
As we speed through the night
Down an open road of lights.
We're trying to get away,
Trying to bridge the distance in our words,
Like we closed the spaces
On the dance floor.
It's easy to move our bodies
And let the music heal our arguments.
I prefer when there is no end in sight.
Just give me one last fight
Rather than fade away
Without a goodbye.
The music is rising
Like my heartbeat.
The memories are starting to blur,
Like staring at a disco ball,
Like a long love that had to grow silent
To grow honest and free.
I hope this ride through night
Never ends
And that the sun
Doesn't burn away
The last trace of a feeling.

## Pages Torn Between Us

I want to tear you
From the seams of my memory.
I want to shred every word
That got lost in translation.
Typos of bad decisions;
Too much frustration and not enough patience,
Like trying to create a work of art
By rushing the process
And having the whole thing
Collapse and shatter.
I want to erase the smiles on the photographs.
I need to draw more spaces between us.
Car rides without talking,
Birthdays missed;
Can you even take a diss?
Or must you flip the problem,
Casually throwing blame, on me
For not saying something sooner?

## Excuses

You say you never knew
How I felt,
But did you even ask?
Don't be mad we never grew.
The painted joy was but a mask.
You're asking for a clue.
Oh, what a heavy task
After the long reflection
I gave to you.
You no longer speak with me,
But instead just pass.
Avoidance is a game I lose.
I'll always be the first to reach out.
You'll always be the last.

# Denial

When you care so much
About people
Who don't show care for you,
You neglect your own values
In the end.

You confront them
And they flip the issue.
You tell them your discomfort
And they never show they miss you.
Words thrown out are simple and blunt;
They say it's only
Your problem to confront.
They don't acknowledge their privilege.
They don't consider,
For a moment,
That you could be right.
They make you have to fight
To be heard, to be regarded as important,
To feel like a part of this friendship
To begin with.
The lies and ignorance;
You feel it,
You see it,
But still they deny
And that hurts deep.

When you care so much,
And you don't want to anymore,
About your friends,
It feels like something
No amount of time apart can mend.

That is a heavy feeling
Without any resolution
But to move forward.
I'd rather attempt to heal
By focusing on what I do have
And focusing on those loved ones
Who chose to stay
Rather than everything that has been lost.

# If People Care

Do they ever think of me
Or am I irrelevant?
They moved on so quickly.
It's as if my absence was welcomed.
If these people care,
They have an odd way of showing it.
Is it easy for them to move on?
Does anyone look back once they're gone?
It's tough to know if people care
When they're so distant in speech,
So cold with emotion.
They're so careful with what they share.
It's tough to know if people care.

## Parting Is All We Know

Parting is all that we know
How to do in the end;
No more texts,
No long goodbyes or hope.
Reaping as we sow;
Tell me what is next?
So long as we still grow,
We'll be polite on the surface.
We forget what we once saved;
Memories bound to fade,
Till our dying days and disputes
Of old are put to rest.

## Just Say It's Over

Sliding away;
There for over a decade
And then gone one day;
You gave much less
Of your time or care
Towards the end.
You did what you do best:
Just hid away and avoided.
That's fine,
But I can't keep patiently waiting
To simply be acknowledged
While other people receive greater attention.
I wish we could've met one last time,
To rightly end things
Or if you could've just said
That the relationship was over.
That clarity would've been better
Than the silence.
That's asking too much
From anyone who lies to themselves,
Which is what we all do at times.
We want so badly to appear tough,
Indifferent, cool, intimidating,
But underneath we're emotional messes.

## Re-defining

We define who we are
Through our relationships.
To lose someone,
Means losing who we once were.
Losing that version of ourselves
Means assuming that great academic work
Doesn't equate to a great job right away;
Means trying and failing and trying
Every day of the week
From nine to five at an office job
And still never quite fitting in.
Uncertainty initially feels terrible,
But it can be an adventure.
It can feel
Like a flight through the night,
To magical lands and places,
Where it isn't silly at all to dream.

## Nonchalant

You're so nonchalant;
Slow like a tide,
Soothing the sand,
Washing away the piles
Of waste, of haste,
Of all the clutter we built up.
Why is it
That even the best relationships
Catch some dust?
Garbage words of the past,
Are those memories that start to rust.
They don't fit
In your exciting, polished world;
The events I cannot part my mind from
No matter how much I think;
No hate or ill wishes;
Just the fact
That our paths
Were meant to divide.
Here we are,
Floating away,
Like balloons in the pale blue sky.
You're so nonchalant,
Restless as a kite,
Breaking to get away;
Striking, colorful,
Never meant to fade.

## Relationship Like Clay

Relationship like clay;
Why do we take something beautiful
And then bend it ugly, misshapen, and twisted?
It's not enough to feel the loss.
We have to destroy the memory
In order to move on with our story.

Some things about a relationship are bad.
It's not everything.
It's not all the time.
So why does everything feel like it was bad?
Because, it's easier to move on that way.
It's harder to remember
That you once cared,
That there was love.
If you remembered everything,
You'd miss it too much.

Relationship like clay;
Create a new shape,
A fresh layer of color,
To move on from the mess you made.

*Chapter 5*

# Reflections Through A Pandemic

THE YEAR 2020 HAS been a year full of strife. There has been a pandemic that changed the way we live our lives, that tore families apart, and that surrounded people with death and despair. There have been too many situations of racial discrimination even amidst the pandemic, showing the world that there is still much more work to do. In response, there have been more protests for the Black Lives Matter movement and more involvement by people to actively make changes instead of just talking about it and letting it trend online. The need for greater awareness in being anti-racist, reflection on possible resolutions for these social issues, and a need to take the re-posting on social media and put it into effective actions has really defined this year of 2020. The pandemic is still ongoing even as I'm writing this section. This year has reminded me the most of endurance, taking each day as it comes, standing up for what you believe in, having faith, taking care of each other, focusing on what I am grateful for, and that love is stronger than all the things that divide people on this earth. The past is not forever, but sometimes it feels that way and sometimes the mistakes of the past are repeated in the present. Writing out all these poems has pushed me to reflect on different stages of my life and shown me how intertwined all our lives are. Without the past that helps shape you into who you are, you can't become who you need to be.

## Conveniences

I'm thankful for conveniences:
A cup of coffee in the morning,
A movie or show
To help me escape,
A book to attract my wandering thoughts,
A meal that makes me feel nourished
And lucky to be alive,
A comfortable bed to sleep on,
Assignments for school to keep my busy,
A phone conversation with a friend,
A few hours filled with drawing
A place I long to see,
A song to excite my soul,
A faith that keeps me strong,
A light that shines at night;
Makes me feel like it's Christmas all year long,
A world that will not break no matter how it is tried
And divided.

## Career Crisis

Whether we're dealing
With losing a job,
Quitting by choice,
Or being let go,
It's never easy.
I want to move forward,
But I keep swinging backwards.
I keep blaming myself
For not being more successful,
For not knowing by now
What my ultimate career goal is.
I've always been lost,
From grade school to everything
That I still face
Even after graduating college.
I know I'm good at some things.
Does that mean they should be my career?

## Love Is On My Mind

I want to find love,
But I'm afraid it'll never arrive.
It's the least of my worries,
But love is on my mind.

How do you date these days,
When lives are at stake?
Isolated, quarantined;
Even before the pandemic,
It was so hard to meet anyone
And stay protective of yourself.

You have to be careful
With your information
On social media
Because you don't always know
Who you are letting into your life.
In person or online,
It's hard to trust anyone these days.
Love feels like a game,
A confusing game that people
Only want to play.

I live in New York
And love seems romantic and easy
On a television screen.
Yet, because New Yorkers move so fast,
We hardly ever stop to meet new people.
We're also taught
To not talk with strangers,
To be independent,
To always be moving,
And to look for the next adventure.

So, it's hard to settle down.
It's rare
To even find love at all.

## Green To The Bone

Green to the bone;
Embers crisp with claws reaching,
Always hungry for more
Until it's taken
All your free will and passion.

Money, money, money;
A dark cloud that never left;
A knife in the back
Just as you got back up again;
It's the mind's cruel defense
To a bit of freedom and authenticity.
Why do we live this way?
We're only ever asking
How much?
Is there an industry for that?
Of course there isn't,
Not until you go out there
Striking with pure fire,
Say "this is who I am and you need to deal,"
And you build whatever you want!

Talent is not always enough
To appease the mind's quaking
And riveting pitfalls.
Understand, I see no other way,
Than to live with a paintbrush,
Making worlds out of the colors;
Than to stand by my pen,
Always raising my voice
Even if the world refuses to listen.

And what about money?
Money is paper;
Money is pressure trying to
Bulldoze me into the ground.
It's a force, sure,
But so am I
And just because it's
Always on the mind,
Doesn't mean
My every thought and action
Points toward its compass.
I'd never be more lost if that happened.

No one just gave me the talent,
The creativity, the time to reflect, and to create.
It never gets easier.
I had to work for it.
I still work for it.
Everyday, I deal with the world's doubts and my own.
People want me to be this and then that,
But never me in my truest sense
In the obscure way that just feels natural to me.

I don't think the rest of the world sees how hard it is.
Their eyes are glinted in green,
Not by choice,
But by conditioning,
By routine,
By pressure they let pummel them.
For the world is cruel and unforgiving when it comes
To a simple dream.

When it comes to "I want,"
Everyone becomes a slave to money
And while it is something we need,
Something that breaks our backs,
And makes the sweat turn into tears,
Money is not my sole motivation in life.
It never will be.

## Capitalism Never Sleeps

Oh capitalism, why won't you sleep?
Look, how NYC traffic has died down!
The roads are clear, the sky more gray,
And people are despairing.
What can I say?

The death toll keeps rising,
But it's not just the United States.
Look at the whole world:
People struggling and people helping,
People dying and people who keep living;
See what their words and kind actions meant.
Did you forget again that it's also Lent?

Oh capitalism, why won't you just call it a night?
No more phone calls throughout my day;
Please no more claimants asking for their money;
No more shallow lies that everything will be okay.
These aggressive emails are piling up
Like dead bodies outside of hospitals,
Where doctors and nurses can only do so much.
It's never enough for you.

I'm tired of my bosses asking for medicals
For their hearings.
Cut the hearings;
Do something daring
Or selfless or caring?
The world is supposed to be on pause,
But the greedy are already dead inside
Because they don't understand human loss.

Just call these cold-blooded corporations *Nosferatu*.
Their greed is what will kill us, not a plague.
This need to make life move so fast
Is what drives us further back into our past.
This job is really not where I want to be.
It's just where I am and I'm grateful;
That doesn't mean I want my time taken, still.

# Toxic Office

Toxic office led by toxic people;
Bosses who demand everything
And give so little respect and benefits;
I feel guilty just saying that
I'll be out of the office for a week
And not giving an elaborate excuse.
I feel anxiety
Just from being a recluse
And not engaging in any office gossip.

It doesn't feel real
To believe that I'm free from this job.
I'm done?
I'm really leaving?
I don't know why,
But I've come to expect disappointment
From most jobs.
I hate that feeling of settling.
Yet, it's what I keep doing
Because I need a job.

## Millennial

Millennial, dirty word;
A fine joke to describe
My generation.

We need answers
And we need them now!
There is no time to waste
Or patience for the old ways
Of toxic mindsets;
Or traditions meant to enslave,
Abuse, silence, or derange
Our voices that can't stop rising.

Protests,
Social media stories on replay,
Hash tags, reposts, and no rest;
Why is the world's humanity in delay?
I'm a millennial drunk on bliss,
But it's not the partying or clubbing
You'd accuse me of missing.
I'm searching for purpose
And I still have yet to find it.

Or rather, I've found meaning
In life at different points,
But all those feelings
Are just aging memories now.
I need something new and important
To be a part of,
To find value in,
To feel worthy of.

Millennial;
Unsatisfied traveler,
Looking for answers in faith,
In drawings,
In long, forgotten books,
In music that screams emotions,
In photographs of the world's past,
In horoscopes, and in astrology;
To find truth is an endless task.

## Social Activism, Social Media

Social media posts
Erupting with conviction;
We can't do all the work
Only on social media,
But it's a start.
It's a place to connect
And voice opinions and support
For what we believe in.
Having a hashtag trend
Or taking part in a challenge
Is not always the same though
As actually being aware of what happened.

Doing the research,
Reading all the details,
And taking action
To change the pattern
Of injustices is necessary;
We need to stop
This cycle of discrimination
So deeply rooted into language,
Education, economics,
Movies, pop culture,
And a history built on slavery.
There are too many echoes of the past
Seeping into the present.
Why are people so hesitant
To change these patterns?
Is it better to act like vultures,
Feasting on human pain?

All Black lives matter,
Justice for Breonna Taylor,
Justice for Oluwatoyin Salau,
Say her name,
Keep saying, keep learning,
Keep caring, and keep fighting.
Keep signing petitions, donating,
Sending emails to demand justice,
And realize that the real work
Doesn't stop or start on social media.

## Uncertainty Blooms

Uncertainty blooms like a new love;
Foreign, different, unfamiliar;
Nothing scares us more
Than finding a joy we can easily lose.

Uncertainty fumes like untamed anger;
Rage balled into a fist,
Knuckles tight, and shaking;
No knowing if it'll be a hit or a miss.
Blank stares void of care,
Words unsaid, and thoughts too blunt
Are what feeds into the great fear:
That we're all alone
With no real home,
Except for the places we decided to claim
For the people we couldn't help loving.

Uncertainty like when
My family came
To the United States;
They left their home and had to start all over;
Everything foreign, strange, and intimidating;
Uncertainty like picking a major in college,
When you have no clue who you are,
Or how you'll fare in a career.

Uncertainty like starting a new job;
You do the best you can,
But something isn't quite right;
You keep trying until you fail;
You keep failing until you succeed.

Uncertainty in the deepest relationships,
Thinking that a friendship of fifteen years
Meant nothing to the other person
Is a slow, poisonous thought
That infects the good memories slowly.

Is it delusion or simple uncertainty
To think that those cherished memories
Will be erased forever
To make room for new moments,
New people who matter?

Uncertainty comes in many shapes,
Like staring at a blank page,
Never knowing what to say,
And feeling overwhelmed with emotions
That are breaking to get out.
There is dreadful uncertainty
In graduating from college
And still not knowing
What the right career path is.
Sometimes, it feels
Like no such place or position exists.

We're all searching for human connection,
Approval, and appreciation
In this sea of social media.
Through instagram stories,
We peer into people's lives
And think we know
What is really going on inside.

Not knowing is the real enemy;
This idea that we're all lost
With nowhere to go;
No point in trying when we feel so low.
I think that fear, doubt, and uncertainty
Are a great abyss we can drown in.
Uncertainty lingers like friendships
That never officially ended,
But the separation occurred
And the distance grew.
Uncertainty blooms like funeral flowers,
Something bright and colorful,
Even though a light has left the world.

## Too Much Thinking

Too much thinking
And not enough action
Is too much drinking,
Consuming all the friction.

Tension;
Heat is building
In my mind, in my doubts
That I don't know
Where I'm going anymore.
All roads lead the same.
Every person has a story;
Same story told in different ways;
Life and death,
Pain and euphoria,
Sweet and sour,
Horizon of our dreams,
And deep abyss of our guilt.

We do not regret bad actions
As much as we loathe
Those words unsaid;
Words that are unbridled and untamed
Still sting
Years after they're spoken.
What we never said
Is sometimes worse, however,
Than the unapologetic words
That were spoken.
Everything in the silence scares us,
Breaks us apart,
And leaves us with wounds
That stay open for years.

## Anytime I Get Sad

Anytime I get sad,
I think of all the little details
In my life that bring joy.
I listen to music
That speaks to my mood.
My mood is always changing
Like the tide,
Like phases of the moon,
Or seasons of the year.
I'm motivated by people
I've never met.
My soul is touched by the people
I've been lucky enough to know.
I search through my library
For a book that satisfies my desire
For beautiful prose and a good story.
I draw until I feel like I've healed.
I write to make the words count.
I walk through the park with my mom
And we talk
And the world doesn't seem
So dark or lonely.

I scroll through social media
And my own problems seem minimal.
When I pray,
I feel relieved and nourished
To not just be focusing on me.
I want so many things out of life
That I sometimes forget the power
Of actually living.

In order to enjoy this life,
All of your dreams
Don't have to come true.
It's more about understanding and finding
Beauty in the mundane.
The ordinary becomes extraordinary
When you take a moment
To treasure little details.

The job you hate is a job
That someone else really needs
And wishes they could have.
The home you made,
Not just the house that you live in,
Is a feeling and a place
That has been robbed from too many.
The same old meals you're eating
Are the greatest nourishment
To those who are starving.
The moment you wake up in the morning
And breathe fresh air
Is a blessing that some people
Will no longer have.
Anytime I get sad,
Thinking of these little details saves me.

## Shoes Not Used

Leather, black,
High-heeled beauties,
Sitting on the shoe rack;
Days pass
And laughter is heard
Throughout the house.

Everyone hears it,
Even the sneaky little mouse.
Voices upstairs and downstairs,
Children playing in the outside world;
People are still speaking and eating.
They're still trying
To get work done.
What about those shoes?
Don't they get a word
Or a few moments in the sun?

Sure, shoes can't talk
Or maybe
People never listen,
But they do use those shoes to walk.
All those years of good old walking
With the same feet
And colorful socks.
The black, leather,
High-heeled shoes
Were proud to be used
By the same feet for all that time.

Now things are changing.
The owner has been very unkind,
Letting the shoes catch some dust.
The owner doesn't really go outside
Or take long bike rides
Like they used to.
Yet, they walk around the house,
Always wearing some pretty blouse,
A pair of black jeans,
And bright, pink lipstick.
Now, wouldn't the shoes go great
With all of that?

This special pair of shoes
Is having an identity crisis!
What is a shoe
If it isn't being used?
All the while,
Its owner lives and breathes
And walks each day.
That is just not right
And the shoes are losing their sight.
Now the shoes are just for decoration;
They remain a relic
Of an older time
Because time has used up all its patience.

## Spring Birthday

My mother's birthday is in spring;
Taurus woman, jovial, tough,
Brown eyes, great wardrobe;
There is nothing stronger than her love.

Wise, caring, and extremely daring;
She also loves the comforts of home
Like candles, great food, sweet scents;
She seems restless these days
Because there's nowhere to roam.

She lost her job in November.
The struggle has been too hard to describe.
So I won't even try,
But I'll always remember
Our late night tradition
Of getting dinner in our city
Each year on her birthday.

Sometimes we'd get Thai food,
Other times a Mediterranean cuisine.
We'd both get dressed up,
Like we were going out to a party.
It never mattered where we went.
As long as we were together,
The time was well spent.

This year is different.
She's unemployed
And we're facing a pandemic.
There is so much sorrow and fear
Mingled with everyday routines.
It's tough to celebrate
When death lingers in the air.
Though, I say the feelings of sadness
Make me crave moments of real happiness.

There is no better way
To celebrate a birthday
Than with a friend
And realize love
Is something that never ends.

## Anxiety, An Old Friend

Anxiety attack;
No time to pack!
We're stuck where we are,
Not lost in our past,
Nor are we moving toward a future.
No one can travel.
We can barely leave our homes.
The only journey that unravels
Is in anxiety filled poems.

Stressful phone calls, rude emails;
I make tons of notes in files,
But it all fails somehow.
Everything is crumbling down.
I'm so confused.
I have no idea what to do
Or why I'm even doing it anymore?

Anxiety attack;
What is it that I lack?
Is it some more knowledge
Of the world
Or not knowing when to stop?
Stop talking bluntly
At important social gatherings.
Stop making mistakes at work.
Stop saying the wrong answers at interviews.
Stop writing stories that no one will read.

I need my dreams to happen now;
Full written books and stories that matter,
Not just flashy fiction and useless chatter.
I don't know how

I can make my dreams turn into reality
When there is such little time to create.
I should have all the time in the world now.
Yet, my hours are still filled
With pointless matters,
Taking orders from people with large egos.
Is there time to filter through the banter
And find something
With long lasting meaning?

## Another Day

This lack of movement
Is driving me insane.
It's too much some days.
Other days, it's just fine.
I'll sleep in on the weekends
And get up early during the week.
It's the same routine
Because I work from home.
That is a blessing for sure,
But it's still uncomfortable.
It makes my stomach stir
To have clients randomly call
After work hours
On my cell phone
And home phone,
Asking for more information
As if I have all the answers.
Sometimes, I have absolutely no clue
What to say to them or what to do.

Just one more day
Is another day closer to the weekend.
Then, I can take time to mend
All the stress
From the week and the fear
That this pandemic
Will never end.
Another day and it may be over.
Another day is actually a luxury
Because these days,
As death tolls rise,
Not everyone gets another day
With family and friends,

Doing the things that they love.
So, another day
Is my way
Of saying thank you to God.

# Earth Day

It's Earth Day;
What can I say?
Nothing will ever change the way
That we destroy
What we love.

A nice stroll through the park
With garbage that doesn't make it
To the trash;
Cigarettes on grass;
Lazy afternoons
With long baths
Where the water just runs wastefully.

It's never enough,
No matter how many resources we have.
We always want more
And isn't that sad?
I think we all forget,
That we don't own Earth.
We just live within it,
Breathing air,
Making homes on this land.

We use its nourishment for our gain.
Yet, even through this Corona Virus,
Human beings perish
While the earth remains strong,
Vibrant, and beautiful.
It will live on without us,
Endure changes, and adapt.
Yet we still think that we own it.

## Reading Through A Crisis

Why do we read?
Everyone has a reason,
A book that they love
Or a story that is pleasing
And simply feels like home.
There is a special book for every season.
I'm not just teasing.
Certain words flow well
At different times in our lives.
Fall feels like *Anne Of Green Gables,*
Or *Frankenstein* or *Wuthering Heights.*

It's so hard to choose a favorite,
But fall is the best season.
Nothing about the changing leaves
Is easy and light.
No, it's a time
Full of depth
And great meaning.

Winter matches
With nothing better than
*The Chronicles of Narnia: The Lion, The Witch and The Wardrobe.*
It combines the magic of this season
With charming characters
And a plot that is very pleasing
To most people
Who are looking for
Something more,
Like talking animals
Or magic in the world.
The world is often
Way too realistic

And dull.
Summer pairs precisely,
Like a pair of focused,
Spectacled eyes,
With the indulgent,
Nostalgic *The Great Gatsby*.
As for spring,
There is no sweeter thing
Than meeting the March sisters
For the first time in *Little Women*.

I read books because of a deep need
To travel the world,
To live in other people's shoes,
To experience everything in life
That I know I'll never actually do.

## Pastries At Martha's

I miss going to Martha's Country Bakery,
Sitting on familiar wooden chairs,
Gazing at rows of pastries:
Strawberry cheesecake, creamy éclairs.
Those are my favorite types of days
When sunlight makes everything
A golden haze.

I miss the warmth of conversations
Between friends
Who can talk about anything;
Kind eyes, big, hearty laughs
And patience
As I asked my friends
"What do you think?"

I asked them about my life,
My job, all the stories I wrote.
I asked them and also listened
To their opinions
And vast knowledge of the world.
Communication, good communication,
Is part of what makes
The world so great.
Being able to talk
With someone you love
For hours
Is an underrated blessing.

# Home

Purple, patterned sheets,
Red, leather Guess purse
Sitting on the printer I never use;
Peacock sketch hanging on the wall,
Unfinished.
It reminds me
Of all the unfinished projects
I have.
Sometimes, I keep things unfinished
In order to preserve them.
It savors the life
And the journey of the piece
A little bit longer.
Once a drawing is finished,
Once a story is told,
The art is no longer
Being created
And that spark is gone.

Home is every Christmas season,
When my family and I
Put up the same old decorations.
No hesitation
Can beat the sensation
Of these traditions;
Opening up
Long, cardboard boxes
That are messily taped,
To find colorful
Christmas ornaments.

Home is every Halloween,
Hanging out at my friend's house,
Baking all kinds of decadent sweets,
And making the effort
To dress up
No mater how old we got.
We would catch up on life
And watch classic, scary movies.

Home is going
To Austin Street
With my friends,
Feeling like these simple and good times
Will never end.

Home is coconut,
Ginger, cassava,
Nutmeg, almond essence, and guava;
Baking in the kitchen
With mom or grandma.
Home is the gift
Of having
An anxious, excited
Siberian husky to come back to.
It never mattered
How fussy the day was.
Home is sitting
In Bryant Park,
Sipping coffee,
Catching up with a friend,
And being surrounded
By green life.
Home amounts
To all the adventures

In New York City
Through the seasons,
Getting out of the house,
Putting up with the subway,
Going to the city for no reason,
But to get away.

Home is not just my house,
But all the houses,
Buildings, and open spaces
That have let me in their doors.
These places have left me
With memories to embrace
When I can no longer
Visit these places.

## Halloween

I used to love Halloween.
Every year,
It felt like a dream;
Jack o' lanterns, black cats,
Candy corn, and witch hats.

Now, it feels so ordinary.
It's almost like adulthood
Robbed me
Of the excitement
That was so natural
In my youth.

Trick-or-treating
Will never be the same.
People will think twice
Before they let their kids
Take candy from strangers,
No matter how nice.
Disease spreads too easily these days.
Horror movies aren't so frightening.
The real terror comes
From turning on the news.
Death and despair
Linger everywhere,
Spreading longer
Than a season or day.

## Fall

Season of change;
All year long I wait.
When fall arrives,
It passes too quickly
Through my life.
It's like a flaming arrow
That is both majestic and bright.
I want to touch it,
But I don't do it
For pure fright
Of getting burned.

Fall is felt in
Gloomy weather, gray skies,
Hot cocoa, and pumpkin pie.
Fall is embraced in
Red scarves, plaid shirts,
Leather jackets, and black skirts.

I look at
Tall, wet, lonesome trees,
Branches bare and twisted,
Outstretched for the longing touch
Of someone to love.
I wander through
Carnivals and smell
Caramel corn.
There are candied apples
That make
My mouth water
With temptation.

I long to find
A dimpled smile
Just as decadent.
New vows of love sediment
As the past haunts but never controls.
Wild emotions rise
From a single day
As fast and changing
As the seasons.

Tombstones remain cold,
Even covered in fallen leaves.
Flowers are dying,
While old wounds are prying.
It's beauty of a different means.

Some days are full of simple comforts:
Soft sunlight sweeping
On dew stricken leaves
Of red, orange, and green.
It's strange how they look
More ravishing
As they fall and die.

Walks through the park with a friend;
Secrets told in late November;
Words that only wind may carry
For the trust of a loved one
Is enough safety to reassure
The mind's pauses and leisure;
Apple cider and the scent of cinnamon,
Nutmeg, cloves,
And spiced gin;

Butternut squash,
Acorns, sweet potato;
Eerie settings with lingering fog;
Broomsticks, black cats, cobblestones;
Lights in the form of
Plastic skeleton bones;
There are so many sites
To behold
As I pass
The old cemeteries,
The costume stores,
Or even if I stay home
And re-read old folklores.
No matter where the adventure calls,
I am never wearied
In this bustling,
Sensual season of fall.

# Husky

You look less like a dog
And more like a wolf;
Husky,
Playful, unpredictable
Siberian husky;
Blue eyes that could get
Anything they want;
You fell off the couch
And almost injured your leg.
That is probably
The first time
I've ever been afraid for you.
I used to be afraid of dogs.
You changed all of that.

You fill the house with warmth.
Though you can be a drama king,
Always asking for more treats
And food to eat,
Though you want attention all the time,
I couldn't imagine
Going through this pandemic
Without your presence.
You make the mornings brighter,
With your barks and striking stares.
You make the afternoons comforting
As you leap onto the couch
And hang out with everyone.
You provide humor,
Love, and excitement.
There is never a dull moment
When you are around, sweet husky.
Sometimes you spy on your humans,
Pasting your ears
To the living room door.
We open the door and you almost
Fall through because of how intently
You were listening to us.
Sometimes, you're impatient
With waiting on us
To let you into the living room.
So, you just push the door
With all your strength
And sneak in
Before anyone can block you.
When no one is looking,
You jump up on the table
And steal a juicy apple
You've been eyeing.

It doesn't matter
What kind of mischief
You do
Because you have most of us
Wrapped around your paws.

## Instagram Eye View

People baking bread,
Memes that urge people
To wear their masks,
Followed by videos and pictures
Of people in public spaces
That are crowded;
People socializing and their faces exposed,
Doing the exact opposite
Of what they've been asked;
Social media challenges gone awry,
Feeling more like games of telephone
Where the meaning
Gets lost in translation
The more that people
Post and re-post.

Sometimes, I have to step away
And focus on something else,
Pretend my life is moving forward
Even though everything feels paused.
Writing stories and penning poems
Has helped me deal
With confusing feelings.
The best comforts I know of
Come from
Being around people I love
Even when I'm socially distancing
From them.
A phone call, a video conversation,
Texting, and reacting to stories on instagram;
It all adds
To making the day
Feel brighter.

## Open Road

The site of an open road,
The feel of wind
Brushing through my hair,
Music playing loud
Like a powerful ode
To the past,
Sweet and sour moments,
And green life everywhere
When I look outside the windows;
That makes me feel
Happy, alive, and adventurous.

That freedom, that space to roam about,
And the connection to nature
Is what life should be;
Not sheltered in a home,
No mater how comfortable
A house actually is.
Sometimes, I'd rather not be alone
To my rambling mind
And frantic thoughts
That convince me
That the best times in my life
Are behind me.
When you can't move forward,
You're stuck and the funny thing
About being stuck,
Is that your nagging thoughts
Finally catch up to you.

## Endurance

Some of the greatest escape
Is through nature:
Taking a swim in a great lake
Or riding a bike through the park,
Where fresh tall trees
Are on both sides of the lane.

We can all be so stifled in our homes,
Pacing back and forth
Through menial issues,
Feeling like we're all alone.

Being immersed in nature
Reminds me how wide
The world is.
I recall walking up a hilly path
To get to Forest Park.
My family and I would walk there often.
We'd bring our dog
And there was some kind of magic
In the simplicity:
The subtle movements,
The sweet, gentle breeze,
All the laughter, and ease;
It was a natural synchronicity.

It's not so easy to escape anymore.
I'm stuck in dreadful normality.
The boring, dull days
Are hinged with fear
That everything with a story
And everyone who wants to tell it
Will disappear.

Our country is going into a recession.
Stores are going out of business.
Everywhere, there is a lot of apprehension.
I stopped looking at the news
Because the clutter of information
Wasn't giving me a clue
About what we're all going to do?
Instead, I found temporary escape.
I listen to music and draw places
And try to make sense
Of all the spaces
That are left in my life.

Though I know
Escape can't last forever,
Nor does it solve problems completely,
I've found that endurance is stronger
And I endure through knowing
I am not alone.
My energy, love, and emotions
Don't just belong to me.
They're meant to be shared.
Thinking about what other people
Are going through,
Keeping a balance in perspective
Of all the struggles,
Losses, and hardships
Is what helps me endure.
It's what helps the world endure:
All these connections
That deepen and flourish

Despite the distance,
Despite disaster, injustice,
Failures, rejections,
Sadness, and imperfections.

www.ingramcontent.com/pod-product-compliance
Lightning Source LLC
Chambersburg PA
CBHW050803160426
43192CB00010B/1623